T0311736

Cambridge Elements ≡

Elements in Philosophy and Logic
edited by
Bradley Armour-Garb
SUNY Albany
Frederick Kroon
The University of Auckland

CLASSICAL FIRST-ORDER LOGIC

Stewart Shapiro
Ohio State University

Teresa Kouri Kissel
Old Dominion University

CAMBRIDGE
UNIVERSITY PRESS

CAMBRIDGE
UNIVERSITY PRESS

University Printing House, Cambridge CB2 8BS, United Kingdom

One Liberty Plaza, 20th Floor, New York, NY 10006, USA

477 Williamstown Road, Port Melbourne, VIC 3207, Australia

314–321, 3rd Floor, Plot 3, Splendor Forum, Jasola District Centre,
New Delhi – 110025, India

103 Penang Road, #05–06/07, Visioncrest Commercial, Singapore 238467

Cambridge University Press is part of the University of Cambridge.

It furthers the University's mission by disseminating knowledge in the pursuit of education, learning, and research at the highest international levels of excellence.

www.cambridge.org
Information on this title: www.cambridge.org/9781108987004
DOI: 10.1017/9781108982009

First published 2022

A catalogue record for this publication is available from the British Library.

ISBN 978-1-108-98700-4 Paperback
ISSN 2516-418X (online)
ISSN 2516-4171 (print)

Classical First-Order Logic
Elements in Philosophy and Logic

DOI: 10.1017/9781108982009
First published online: April 2022

Stewart Shapiro
Ohio State University
Teresa Kouri Kissel
Old Dominion University
Author for correspondence: Teresa Kouri Kissel, tkouri@odu.edu

Abstract: One is often said to be reasoning well when one is reasoning logically. Many attempts to say what logical reasoning is have been proposed, but one commonly proposed system is classical first-order logic. This Element will examine the basics of classical first-order logic and discuss some surrounding philosophical issues. The first half of the Element develops a language for the system, as well as a proof theory and model theory. The authors provide theorems about the system they developed, such as unique readability and the Lindenbaum lemma. They also discuss the meta-theory for the system, and provide several results there, including sketching a proof of the soundness and completeness theorems. The second half of the Element compares classical first-order logic to other systems: classical higher-order logic, intuitionistic logic, and several paraconsistent logics which reject the law of ex *falso quodlibet*.

Keywords: classical logic, first-order logic, model theory, proof theory, meta-theory higher-order logic, intuitionistic logic, paraconsistent logic

ISBNs: 9781108987004 (PB), 9781108982009 (OC)
ISSNs: 2516-418X (online), 2516-4171 (print)

Contents

1 Introduction

Logic surely has something to do with reasoning. We say that someone has reasoned poorly about something if they have not reasoned logically, or that an argument is bad because it is not logically valid. There has been much speculation over just what types of logical systems are appropriate for guiding deductive reasoning. Some have suggested that classical first-order logic is the ideal for guiding reasoning (for example, see Quine (1986), Resnik (1996) or Rumfitt (2015)).[1] Classical first-order logic has occasionally been dubbed "the one true logic."

Though there is much debate about the underlying issues, it is safe to say that classical first-order logic has been prevalent in mathematics and philosophy over the past century or so. There are good reasons for this. Classical first-order logic has rules which are more or less intuitive, and it is surprisingly simple given its strength. Plus, it is both sound and complete.[2] As is common in philosophy, however, there is no consensus on the primary status of classical first-order logic. As indicated in Section 6, there are certain expressive limitations to first-order logic and, as indicated in the later sections (7-9), there are serious, well-developed rivals to classical logic.

This Element will examine classical first-order logic and then provide a more thorough understanding of it by exploring some alternative logics. In the first half, we provide the details of classical first-order logic. Then, we consider three alternatives to the system we develop: classical higher-order logic (Section 7), intuitionistic logic (Section 8), and para-consistent logics (Section 9).[3]

CLASSICAL FIRST-ORDER LOGIC

2 Formal System

For our purposes, a logic includes a formal language and a deductive system and/or a model-theoretic semantics.[4] A formal language is like a natural

---

[1] When discussing critical thinking and argument analysis, classical first-order logic, is usually, but not always, the starting point. See, for example, Stebbing (1939) and Woods (2021).

[2] We say what this means below.

[3] There are a number of alternatives to classical first-order logic that we will not have space to cover here. In particular, we omit modal logics (see Marcus (1995), for example) and substructural logics (see Restall (2000), amongst others).

[4] Sections 2-6 are based on Shapiro and Kouri Kissel (2020). More complete proofs and proof sketches can be found there, or in most textbooks for formal logic. We include here only a few of the complete proofs: those that are required to prove unique readability, as an example of how proofs often go, and a proof of theorem 4.5 (The rule of Cut) Not all logics have both a deductive system and model theory, but we will develop both for classical first-order logic here.

language, such as English, Japanese, or Swahili, but with explicit and simple rules of composition. It has terms and components which come together in a grammatical way. The deductive system is meant to capture reasoning presented in the language. The model theory gives meanings to the terms in the language, and tells us which propositions are true in various interpretations.

Section 3 develops a formal language with a rigorous syntax and grammar. The formal language is a recursively defined collection of strings on a fixed alphabet. Items in the formal language do not mean anything on their own – they need the deductive system and model theory to give them meaning. Some items correspond to items in natural language, and the deductive system and model theory are designed to preserve this correspondence, at least approximately. An *argument* is a non-empty collection of sentences in the formal language, one of which is designated to be the *conclusion*. The other sentences (if any) in an argument are its *premises*.

Section 4 sets up a deductive system for the language, in the spirit of natural deduction. An argument is *derivable* if there is a deduction from some or all of its premises to its conclusion. Section 5 provides a model-theoretic semantics. An argument is *valid* if there is no interpretation (in the semantics) in which its premises are all true and its conclusion false. This reflects the long-standing view that a valid argument is truth-preserving.

In Section 6, we explore the relationship between the deductive system and the model-theoretic semantics. We will be interested mostly in the relationship between derivability and validity. We sketch two important theorems. The first, *soundness*, will show that no deduction can start with a true premise and end with a false conclusion. So, if an argument is derivable, then it is valid. Proving this shows that deductions preserve truth. The second, *completeness*, is the converse of soundness. It shows that if an argument is valid, then it is derivable. This demonstrates that there are "enough deductions": all valid arguments are derivable. We also briefly indicate other features of the logic, some of which are corollaries to soundness and completeness.

3 Language

Here we develop the basics of the formal language we will use for classical logic. As noted, a formal language is a recursively defined set of strings on a fixed alphabet. Some parts of the formal language correspond to some parts of natural language. This correspondence is not really a part of the formal language, but noting these correspondences can help motivate the system.

3.1 Building Blocks

We start with analogues of *singular terms*, sometimes just called *terms*. These are linguistic items whose function is to denote a person or object. We assume a stock of *individual constants*. These are lower-case letters, near the beginning of the Roman alphabet, with or without numerical subscripts:

$a, a_1, b_{23}, c, d_{22}$, etc.

Constants are an analogue of proper names. We allow ourselves an infinity of individual constants. Each constant is a single character, and so individual constants do not have an internal syntax. Thus, we have an infinite alphabet.[5]

There are two roles that constants play. One is like that of proper names, where a constant denotes a specific object or person (in each interpretation). The other is to denote specific, but unspecified (or arbitrary), objects and persons.[6]

We also assume a stock of *individual variables*. These are lower-case letters, near the end of the alphabet, with or without numerical subscripts:

w, x, y_{12}, z, z_4, etc.

Variables are used to express generality. In ordinary language, some uses of pronouns play the latter role, as in "When a dog is angry, it growls."[7]

We next introduce *function symbols*. These allow complex terms corresponding to: "5 + 3" and "the Marvel character played by Chadwick Boseman," or terms containing variables, like "the sister of x" and "x/y." Function symbols are lower-case letters, near the middle of the alphabet:

f, g, h, etc.

Each function has an arity, that is, the number of arguments it takes.

We now give a recursive definition of the *terms* of the language:

1. All individual constants and all variables are terms.
2. If $t_1, \ldots t_n$ are terms and f is an *n*-place function symbol, then $ft_1 \ldots t_n$ is a term.
3. That's all folks: every term is constructed in accordance with (1) and (2).

A term is *closed* if it contains no variables.

For each natural number n, we introduce a stock of n–place *predicate letters*. These are upper-case letters at the beginning or middle of the alphabet.

---

[5] This could be avoided by taking a constant like d_{22}, for example, to consist of three characters, a lowercase "d" followed by a pair of subscript "2"s.

[6] Some authors use (free) variables for this role; others use different symbols for this, sometimes called "individual parameters."

[7] Another use of pronouns is to denote a specific object or person, as supplied by the context. The formal language has no analogue of this.

A superscript indicates the number of places, and there may or may not be a subscript. For example, A^3, B_2^3, D^3, etc, are three-place predicate letters. We often omit the superscript when no confusion will result. We also add a special two-place predicate symbol "=" for identity.

Zero-place predicate letters are sometimes called "sentence letters." They correspond to freestanding sentences whose internal structure does not matter. One-place predicate letters, called "monadic predicate letters," correspond to linguistic items denoting properties, adjectives, or common nouns like "woman," "large," or "prime number." Two-place predicate letters, called "binary predicate letters," correspond to linguistic items denoting binary relations, like "is a parent of" or "is shinier than." Three-place predicate letters correspond to three-place relations, like "lies on a straight line between." And so on.

The *non-logical terminology* of the language consists of its individual constants and predicate letters. The symbol "=", for identity, is not a non-logical symbol. In taking identity to be logical, we provide explicit treatment for it in the deductive system and in the model-theoretic semantics. Most authors do the same, but there is some controversy over the issue (see Quine (1986) Chapter 5). If K is a set of constants and predicate letters, then we give the fundamentals of a language $\mathcal{L}1K=$ built on this set of non-logical terminology. It may be called the *first-order language with identity* on K. A similar language that lacks the symbol for identity (or which takes identity to be non-logical) may be called $\mathcal{L}1K$, the *first-order language without identity* on K.

3.2 Atomic Formulas

If V is an n-place predicate letter in K, and $t_1, \ldots, t_n$ are terms of K, then $Vt_1 \ldots t_n$ is an *atomic formula* of $\mathcal{L}1K=$. Examples of atomic formulas include:

$P^4xaab, C^1x, C^1a, D^0, A^3aba.$

The last one is an analogue of a statement that a certain relation (A) holds between the objects (a, b, a). If t_1 and t_2 are terms, then $t_1 = t_2$ is also an atomic formula of $\mathcal{L}1K=$. It corresponds to an assertion that t_1 is identical to t_2.

If an atomic formula has no variables, then it is called an *atomic sentence*. If it does have variables, it is called *open*. In the above list of examples, the first and second are open; the rest are atomic sentences.

3.3 Compound Formulas

The final items of the lexicon are:

$\neg, \wedge, \vee, \rightarrow, \forall, \exists, (,)$

We give a recursive definition of a *formula* of $\mathcal{L}1K=$:

1. All atomic formulas of $\mathcal{L}1K=$ are formulas of $\mathcal{L}1K=$.
2. If θ is a formula of $\mathcal{L}1K=$, then so is $\neg\theta$.

A formula corresponding to $\neg\theta$ roughly "says" that it is not the case that θ. The symbol "$\neg$" is called "negation," and is a unary connective.

3. If θ and ψ are formulas of $\mathcal{L}1K=$, then so is $(\theta \wedge \psi)$.

The wedge "$\wedge$" corresponds to the English "and" (when "and" is used to connect sentences). So $(\theta \wedge \psi)$ can be read "θ and ψ." The formula $(\theta \wedge \psi)$ is called the "conjunction" of θ and ψ.

4. If θ and ψ are formulas of $\mathcal{L}1K=$, then so is $(\theta \vee \psi)$.

The symbol "$\vee$" corresponds to "either ... or ... or both," so $(\theta \vee \psi)$ can be read "θ or ψ." The formula $(\theta \vee \psi)$ is called the "disjunction" of θ and ψ.

5. If θ and ψ are formulas of $\mathcal{L}1K=$, then so is $(\theta \rightarrow \psi)$.

The arrow "$\rightarrow$" roughly corresponds to "if ... then ... ," so $(\theta \rightarrow \psi)$ can be read "if θ then ψ" or "θ only if ψ."

   The symbols "$\wedge$," "$\vee$," and "$\rightarrow$" are called "binary connectives," since they serve to "connect" two formulas into one. Some authors introduce $(\theta \leftrightarrow \psi)$ as an abbreviation of $((\theta \rightarrow \psi) \wedge (\psi \rightarrow \theta))$. The symbol "$\leftrightarrow$" is an analogue of the locution "if and only if."

6. If θ is a formula of $\mathcal{L}1K=$ and v is a variable, then $\forall v\theta$ is a formula of $\mathcal{L}1K=$.

The symbol "$\forall$" is called a *universal quantifier*, and is an analogue of "for all"; so $\forall v\theta$ can be read "for all v, θ."

7. If θ is a formula of $\mathcal{L}1K=$ and v is a variable, then $\exists v\theta$ is a formula of $\mathcal{L}1K=$.

The symbol "$\exists$" is called an *existential quantifier*, and is an analogue of "there exists" or "there is"; so $\exists v\theta$ can be read "there is a v such that θ."

8. That's all folks: all formulas are constructed in accordance with rules (1)–(7).

   Clause (8) allows us to do inductions on the complexity of formulas. If a certain property holds of the atomic formulas and is closed under the operations presented in clauses (2)–(7), then the property holds of all formulas. Here is a simple example:

Theorem 3.1 *Every formula of $\mathcal{L}1K=$ has the same number of left and right parentheses. Moreover, each left parenthesis corresponds to a unique right parenthesis, which occurs to the right of the left parenthesis. Similarly, each* *right parenthesis corresponds to a unique left parenthesis, which occurs to the left of the given right parenthesis. If a parenthesis occurs between a matched pair of parentheses, then its mate also occurs within that matched pair. In other words, parentheses that occur within a matched pair are themselves matched.*

Proof. By clause (8), every formula is built up from the atomic formulas using clauses (2)–(7). The atomic formulas have no parentheses. Parentheses are introduced only in clauses (3)–(5), and each time they are introduced as a matched set. So at any stage in the construction of a formula, the parentheses are paired off.

We next define the notion of an occurrence of a variable being *free* or *bound* in a formula. A variable that immediately follows a quantifier (as in "$\forall x$" and "$\exists y$") is neither free nor bound. We do not even think of those as occurrences of the variable. All variables that occur in an atomic formula are free. If a variable occurs free in θ or in ψ, then that same occurrence is free in $\neg\theta, (\theta \wedge \psi), (\theta \vee \psi)$, and $(\theta \rightarrow \psi)$. The same goes for bound variables. That is, the (unary and binary) connectives do not change the status of variables that occur in them. All occurrences of the variable v in θ are bound in $\forall v\theta$ and $\exists v\theta$. Any *free* occurrences of v in θ are bound by the initial quantifier. All other variables that occur in θ are free or bound in $\forall v\theta$ and $\exists v\theta$, as they are in θ.

For example, in the formula $(\exists x(Axy \vee Bx) \wedge Bx)$, the occurrences of "$x$" in Axy and in the first Bx are bound by the quantifier. The occurrence of "y" and the last occurrence of "x" are free. In $\forall x(Ax \rightarrow \exists xBx)$, the "$x$" in Ax is bound by the initial universal quantifier, while the other occurrence of x is bound by the existential quantifier. The above syntax allows this "double-binding." Although it does not create any ambiguities (see below), we will avoid such formulas, as a matter of taste and clarity.

The syntax also allows so-called vacuous binding, as in $\forall xBc$. This, too, will be avoided in what follows. Some treatments of logic rule out vacuous binding and double binding as a matter of syntax. That simplifies some of the treatments below and complicates others.

Free variables correspond to placeholders, while bound variables are used to express generality. If a formula has no free variables, then it is called a *sentence*. If a formula has free variables, it is called *open*.

3.4 Features of the Syntax

Before turning to the deductive system and semantics, we mention a few features of the language as developed so far. This helps draw the contrast between formal languages and natural languages like English.

We assume at the outset that all of the categories are disjoint. For example, no connective is also a quantifier or a variable, and the non-logical terms are not also parentheses or connectives. Also, the items within each category are distinct. For example, the sign for disjunction does not do double-duty as the negation symbol, and, perhaps more significantly, no two-place predicate is also a one-place predicate.

One difference between natural languages like English and formal languages like $\mathcal{L}1K=$ is that the latter are not supposed to have any ambiguities. The policy that the different categories of symbols do not overlap, and that no symbol does double-duty, avoids the kind of ambiguity, sometimes called "equivocation," that occurs when a single word has two meanings: "I've got a bat in my garage" (a piece of baseball equipment or a flying mammal?). But there are other kinds of ambiguity. Consider the English sentence:

Mohammed is tall and Xenia is smart or James is silly.

It can mean that Mohammed is tall and either Xenia is smart or James is silly, or else it can mean that either both Mohammed is tall and Xenia is smart, or else James is silly. An ambiguity like this, due to different ways to parse the same sentence, is sometimes called an "amphiboly." If our formal language did not have the parentheses in it, it would have amphibolies. For example, there would be a "formula" $A \wedge B \vee C$. Is this supposed to be $((A \wedge B) \vee C)$, or is it $(A \wedge (B \vee C))$? The parentheses resolve what would be an amphiboly.

Can we be sure that there are no other amphibolies in our language? That is, can we be sure that each formula of $\mathcal{L}1K=$ can be put together in only one way? The answer is yes, and our next task is to show this.

Let us temporarily use the term "unary marker" for the negation symbol $(\neg)$ or a quantifier followed by a variable (e.g., $\forall x, \exists z$).

Lemma 3.2 *Each formula consists of a string of zero or more unary markers followed by either an atomic formula or a formula produced using a binary connective, via one of clauses (3)–(5).*

Proof. We proceed by induction on the complexity of the formula or, in other words, on the number of formation rules that are applied. The Lemma clearly holds for atomic formulas. Let n be a natural number, and suppose that the Lemma holds for any formula constructed from n or fewer instances of clauses (2)–(7). Let θ be a formula constructed from $n+1$ instances. The Lemma holds if the last clause used to construct θ was either (3), (4), or (5). If the last clause used to construct θ was (2), then θ is $\neg\psi$. Since ψ was constructed with n instances of the rule, the Lemma holds for ψ (by the induction hypothesis), and so it holds for θ. Similar reasoning shows the Lemma to hold for θ if the last clause was (6) or (7). By clause (8), this exhausts the cases, and so the Lemma holds for θ, by induction.

Lemma 3.3 *If a formula θ contains a left parenthesis, then it ends with a right parenthesis, which matches the leftmost left parenthesis in θ.*

Proof. This proof also proceeds by induction on the number of instances of (2)–(7) used to construct the formula. Clearly, the Lemma holds for atomic formulas, since they have no parentheses. Suppose, then, that the Lemma holds for formulas constructed with n or fewer instances of (2)–(7), and let θ be constructed with $n + 1$ instances. If the last clause applied was (3)–(5), then the Lemma holds since θ itself begins with a left parenthesis and ends with the matching right parenthesis. If the last clause applied was (2), then θ is $\neg\psi$, and the induction hypothesis applies to ψ. Similarly, if the last clause applied was (6) or (7), then θ consists of a quantifier, a variable, and a formula to which we can apply the induction hypothesis. It follows that the Lemma holds for θ.

Lemma 3.4 *Each formula contains at least one atomic formula.*

Proof. The proof again proceeds by induction on the number of instances of (2)–(7) used to construct the formula.

Theorem 3.5 *Let α, β be nonempty sequences of characters on our alphabet, such that $\alpha\beta$ (i.e., α followed by β) is a formula. Then α is not a formula.*

Proof. If α contains a left parenthesis, then the right parenthesis that matches the leftmost left parenthesis in $\alpha\beta$ comes at the end of $\alpha\beta$, and so the matching right parenthesis is in β. So, α has more left parentheses than right parentheses. By Theorem 3.1, α is not a formula. So now suppose that α does not contain any left parentheses. By Lemma 3.2, $\alpha\beta$ consists of a string of zero or more unary markers followed by either an atomic formula or a formula produced using a binary connective, via one of clauses (3)–(5). If the latter formula was produced via one of clauses (3)–(5), then it begins with a left parenthesis. Since α does not contain any parentheses, it must be a string of unary markers. But then α does not contain any atomic formulas, and so by Lemma 3.4, α is not a formula. The only case left is where $\alpha\beta$ consists of a string of unary markers followed by an atomic formula, either in the form $t_1 = t_2$ or $Pt_1 \ldots t_n$. Again, if α just consisted of unary markers, it would not be a formula, and so α must consist of the unary markers that start $\alpha\beta$, followed by either t_1 by itself, $t_1 = $ by itself, or a predicate letter P, and perhaps some (but not all) of the terms $t_1, \ldots, t_n$. In the first two cases, α does not contain an atomic formula, by the policy that the categories do not overlap. Since P is an n-place predicate letter, by the policy that the predicate letters are distinct, P is not an m-place predicate letter for any $m \neq n$. So the part of α that consists of P followed by the terms is not an atomic formula. In all of these cases, then, α does not contain an atomic formula. By Lemma 3.4, α is not a formula.

These theorems are enough to show that there is no amphiboly in our language. Though just an indication of how the proof goes is provided here, the reader can find the complete proof in Shapiro and Kouri Kissel (2020).

Theorem 3.6 *Let θ be any formula of $\mathcal{L}1K=$. If θ is not atomic, then there is one and only one among (2)–(7) that was the last clause applied to construct θ. That is, θ could not be produced by two different clauses. Moreover, no formula produced by clauses (2)–(7) is atomic.*

Proof. This proof considers each of clauses (2)–(7) in turn to show there is no amphiboly for any of them. By Clause (8), either θ is atomic or it was produced by one of clauses (2)–(7). Thus, the first symbol in θ must be either a predicate letter, a term, a unary marker, or a left parenthesis. If the first symbol in θ is a predicate letter or term, then θ is atomic. In this case, θ was not produced by any of (2)–(7), since all such formulas begin with something other than a predicate letter or term. If the first symbol in θ is a negation sign "¬," then θ was produced by clause (2), and not by any other clause (since the other clauses produce formulas that begin with either a quantifier or a left parenthesis). Similarly, if θ begins with a universal quantifier, then it was produced by clause (6), and not by any other clause, and if θ begins with an existential quantifier, then it was produced by clause (7), and not by any other clause. The only case left is where θ begins with a left parenthesis. In this case, it must have been produced by one of (3)–(5), and not by any other clause. We only need to rule out the possibility that θ was produced by more than one of (3)–(5). To take an example, suppose that θ was produced by (3) and (4). Then θ is $(\psi_1 \wedge \psi_2)$ and θ is also $(\psi_3 \vee \psi_4)$, where ψ_1, ψ_2, ψ_3, and ψ_4 are themselves formulas. That is, $(\psi_1 \wedge \psi_2)$ is the very same formula as $(\psi_3 \vee \psi_4)$. By Theorem 3.5, ψ_1 cannot be a proper part of ψ_3, nor can ψ_3 be a proper part of ψ_1. So ψ_1 must be the same formula as ψ_3. But then "$\wedge$" must be the same symbol as "$\vee$," and this contradicts the policy that each of the symbols are different. So θ was not produced by both Clause (3) and Clause (4). Similar reasoning takes care of the other combinations.

This result is sometimes called "unique readability." It shows that each formula is produced from the atomic formulas via the various clauses in exactly one way. If θ was produced by clause (2), then its *main connective* is the initial "¬." If θ was produced by clauses (3), (4), or (5), then its *main connective* is the introduced "$\wedge$," "$\vee$," or "$\rightarrow$," respectively. If θ was produced by clauses

(6) or (7), then its *main connective* is the initial quantifier. We apologize for the tedious details. We included them to indicate the level of precision and rigor for the syntax.

4 Deduction

We now introduce a *deductive system, D,* for our languages. As above, we define an *argument* to be a non-empty collection of sentences in the formal language, one of which is designated to be the *conclusion*. If there are any other sentences in the argument, they are its *premises*. We use "Γ," "Γ'," "Γ_1," etc., to range over sets of formulas, and we use the letters "ϕ," "ψ," "θ," uppercase or lowercase, with or without subscripts, to range over single formulas. We write "Γ, Γ'" for the union of Γ and Γ', and "Γ, ϕ" for the union of Γ with $\{\phi\}$.

We write an argument in the form $\langle \Gamma, \phi \rangle$, where Γ is a set of sentences, the premises, and ϕ is a single sentence, the conclusion. Remember that Γ may be empty. We write $\Gamma \vdash \phi$ to indicate that ϕ is deducible from Γ, or, in other words, that the argument $\langle \Gamma, \phi \rangle$ is deducible in D. We may write $\Gamma \vdash_D \phi$ to indicate the deductive system D. We write $\vdash \phi$ or $\vdash_D \phi$ to indicate that ϕ can be deduced (in D) from the empty set of premises. The rules in D are chosen to match inferential relations concerning the English analogues of the logical terminology in the language.

We define the deducibility relation by recursion. We start with a rule of assumptions:

- (As) If ϕ is a member of Γ, then $\Gamma \vdash \phi$.

We thus have that $\{\phi\} \vdash \phi$; each premise follows from itself. We next present two clauses for each connective and quantifier. The clauses indicate how to "introduce" and "eliminate" sentences in which each symbol is the main connective.

First, recall that "$\wedge$" is an analogue of the English connective "and." Intuitively, one can deduce a sentence in the form $(\theta \wedge \psi)$ if one has deduced θ and one has deduced ψ. Conversely, one can deduce θ from $(\theta \wedge \psi)$, and one can deduce ψ from $(\theta \wedge \psi)$:

- ($\wedge$I) If $\Gamma_1 \vdash \theta$ and $\Gamma_2 \vdash \psi$, then $\Gamma_1, \Gamma_2 \vdash (\theta \wedge \psi)$.
- ($\wedge$E) If $\Gamma \vdash (\theta \wedge \psi)$, then $\Gamma \vdash \theta$; and if $\Gamma \vdash (\theta \wedge \psi)$, then $\Gamma \vdash \psi$.

The name "($\wedge$I)" stands for "$\wedge$-introduction"; "($\wedge$E)" stands for "$\wedge$-elimination."

Since the symbol "$\vee$" corresponds to the English "or," $(\theta \vee \psi)$ should be deducible from θ, and $(\theta \vee \psi)$ should also be deducible from ψ:

- (∨I) If Γ ⊢ θ, then Γ ⊢ (θ ∨ ψ); if Γ ⊢ ψ, then Γ ⊢ (θ ∨ ψ).

The elimination rule for ∨ is a bit more complicated. Suppose that "θ or ψ" is true. Suppose also that φ follows from θ and that φ follows from ψ. One can reason that if θ is true, then φ is true. If instead ψ is true, we still have that φ is true. So, either way, φ must be true.

- (∨E) If Γ_1 ⊢ (θ ∨ ψ), Γ_2, θ ⊢ φ and Γ_3, ψ ⊢ φ, then $\Gamma_1, \Gamma_2, \Gamma_3$ ⊢ φ.

For the next clauses, recall that the symbol "→" is an analogue of the English "if … then …" construction. If one knows, or assumes, (θ → ψ) and also knows, or assumes θ, then one can conclude ψ. Conversely, if one deduces ψ from an assumption θ, then one can conclude that (θ → ψ).

- (→I) If Γ, θ ⊢ ψ, then Γ ⊢ (θ → ψ).
- (→E) If Γ_1 ⊢ (θ → ψ) and Γ_2 ⊢ θ, then Γ_1, Γ_2 ⊢ ψ.

This elimination rule is sometimes called "modus ponens." In some logic texts, the introduction rule is proved as a "deduction theorem."

Our next clauses are for the negation sign, "¬." The underlying idea is that a sentence ψ is inconsistent with its negation ¬ψ; they cannot both be true. We call a pair of sentences ψ, ¬ψ *contradictory opposites*. If one can deduce such a pair from an assumption θ, then one can conclude that θ is false, or, in other words, one can conclude ¬θ.

- (¬I) If Γ_1, θ ⊢ ψ and Γ_2, θ ⊢ ¬ψ, then Γ_1, Γ_2 ⊢ ¬θ.

By (As), we have that {A, ¬A} ⊢ A and {A, ¬A} ⊢ ¬A. So by (¬I) we have that A ⊢ ¬¬A. However, we do not have the converse yet. Intuitively, ¬¬θ corresponds to "it is not the case that it is not the case that θ." One might think that this last is equivalent to θ, and we have a rule to that effect:

- (DNE) If Γ ⊢ ¬¬θ, then Γ ⊢ θ.

The name (DNE) stands for "double-negation elimination." There is some controversy over this inference. In particular, *intuitionistic logic* does not sanction the inference in question (see Dummett (2000) and Section 8 below). Depending on the intuitionist you look at, their motivations vary widely. But some, at least, hold that in order for a sentence to be true, we need to be able to prove it. This requires, for example, that for each true sentence, we have a proof procedure available for it. Generally, just because we can prove a negation is false (and so prove a double negated claim), this does not imply that we can prove that the unnegated sentence is true. The method of proof in each case is very different, and we cannot be guaranteed to have a proof of A, say, just because we have a proof of $\neg\neg A$. So, intuitionistic logics do not allow (DNE) as a rule.

To illustrate the parts of the deductive system D presented thus far, we show that $\vdash (A \lor \neg A)$:

    i. $\{\neg(A \lor \neg A), A\} \vdash \neg(A \lor \neg A)$, by (As).

    ii. $\{\neg(A \lor \neg A), A\} \vdash A$, by (As).

    iii. $\{\neg(A \lor \neg A), A\} \vdash (A \lor \neg A)$, by ($\lor$I), from (ii).

    iv. $\{\neg(A \lor \neg A)\} \vdash \neg A$, by ($\neg$I), from (i) and (iii).

    v. $\{\neg(A \lor \neg A), \neg A\} \vdash \neg(A \lor \neg A)$, by (As).

    vi. $\{\neg(A \lor \neg A), \neg A\} \vdash \neg A$, by (As).

    vii. $\{\neg(A \lor \neg A), \neg A\} \vdash (A \lor \neg A)$, by ($\lor$I), from (vi).

    viii. $\{\neg(A \lor \neg A)\} \vdash \neg\neg A$, by ($\neg$I), from (v) and (vii).

    ix. $\vdash \neg\neg(A \lor \neg A)$, by ($\neg$I), from (iv) and (viii).

    x. $\vdash (A \lor \neg A)$, by (DNE), from (ix).

The principle $(\theta \lor \neg\theta)$ is sometimes called the *law of excluded middle*. Like (DNE), it is not valid in intuitionistic logic. Some sentences which have the form of (LEM) will not be provable for the intuitionist. For example, we cannot prove "The Goldbach conjecture is true or the Goldbach conjecture is false," since a proof of a disjunction would require us to be able to prove one disjunct, and we do not know which of those disjuncts is true.

Let $\theta, \neg\theta$ be a pair of contradictory opposites, and let ψ be any sentence at all. By (As) we have $\theta, \neg\theta, \neg\psi \vdash \theta$ and $\theta, \neg\theta, \neg\psi \vdash \neg\theta$. So, by ($\neg$I), $\theta, \neg\theta \vdash \neg\neg\psi$. So, by (DNE) we have $\theta, \neg\theta \vdash \psi$. That is, anything at all follows from a pair of contradictory opposites. Some logicians introduce a rule to codify a similar inference:

If $\Gamma_1 \vdash \theta$ and $\Gamma_2 \vdash \neg\theta$, then, for any sentence $\psi, \Gamma_1, \Gamma_2 \vdash \psi$.

The inference is sometimes called *ex falso quodlibet* (EFQ) or, more colorfully, *explosion*. Some call it "$\neg$-elimination," but perhaps this stretches the notion of "elimination" a bit. We do not officially include (EFQ) as a separate rule in D, but, as will be indicated below (Theorem 4.4), each instance of it is derivable in our system D. Some logicians object to this inference (see Section 9). Some of those logicians hold that in an acceptable argument, the premises must be *relevant* to the conclusion. So, for example, they find inferences from "2+2=5" to "snow is white" to be problematic, since the content of the premise (2+2=5) played no actual role in deriving the conclusion (snow is white). Inferences where the premises have no relation to the conclusion can seem intuitively problematic, since they are very far from how we reason in everyday life.

The next items are the clauses for the quantifiers. Let θ be a formula, v a variable, and t a term (i.e., a variable, function, or a constant). Then define $\theta(v|t)$ to be the result of substituting t for each *free* occurrence of v in θ. So, if θ is $(Qx \wedge \exists xPxy)$, then $\theta(x|c)$ is $(Qc \wedge \exists xPxy)$. The last occurrence of x is not free.

A sentence of the form $\forall v\theta$ is an analogue of the English "for every v, θ holds." So one should be able to infer $\theta(v|t)$ from $\forall v\theta$ for any closed term t.

- ($\forall$E) If $\Gamma \vdash \forall v\theta$, then $\Gamma \vdash \theta(v|t)$, for any closed term t.

The idea here is that if $\forall v\theta$ is true, then θ should hold of t, no matter what t is.

The introduction rule for the universal quantifier is a bit more complicated. Suppose that a sentence $\theta(v|c)$ contains an individual constant c, and that $\theta(v|c)$ has been deduced from a set of premises Γ. If c does not occur in any member of Γ, nor in θ, then $\theta(v|c)$ will hold no matter which object c may denote. That is, $\forall v\theta$ follows.

- ($\forall$I) For any constant c, if $\Gamma \vdash \theta(c|t)$, then $\Gamma \vdash \forall v\theta$, provided that c does not occur in Γ or θ.

This rule ($\forall I$) corresponds to a common inference in mathematics. Suppose that a mathematician says, "let n be a natural number" and goes on to show that n has a certain property P, without assuming anything about n (except that it is a natural number). She then reminds the reader that n is "arbitrary," and concludes that P holds for *all* natural numbers. The condition that the term t not occur in any premise is what guarantees that it is indeed "arbitrary." It could be any object, and so anything we conclude about it holds for any object.

The existential quantifier is an analogue of the English expression "there exists," or perhaps just "there is." If we have established (or assumed) that a given object t has a given property, then it follows that there is something that has that property.

- ($\exists$I) For any closed term t, if $\Gamma \vdash \theta(v|t)$, then $\Gamma \vdash \exists v\theta$.

The elimination rule for $\exists$ is not as simple:

- ($\exists$E) For any constant c, if $\Gamma_1 \vdash \exists v\theta$, and $\Gamma_2, \theta(v|c) \vdash \phi$, then $\Gamma_1, \Gamma_2 \vdash \phi$, provided that c does not occur in ϕ, Γ_2, or θ.

This elimination rule also corresponds to a common inference. Suppose that a mathematician assumes or somehow concludes that there is a natural number with a given property P. She then says, "let n be such a natural number, so that Pn," and goes on to establish a sentence ϕ, which does not mention the number n. If the derivation of ϕ does not invoke anything about n (other than the assumption that it has the given property P), then n could have been any number that has the property P. That is, n is an *arbitrary* number with property P. Since ϕ does not mention n, it follows from the assertion that something has property P. The provisions added to ($\exists$E) are to guarantee that c is "arbitrary."[8]

The final items are the rules for the identity sign "=." The introduction rule is about as simple as can be:

- (=I) $\Gamma \vdash t = t$, where t is any closed term.

This "inference" corresponds to the truism that everything is identical to itself. The elimination rule corresponds to a principle that if a is identical to b, then anything true of a is also true of b.

- (=E) For any closed terms t_1 and t_2, if $\Gamma_1 \vdash t_1 = t_2$, and $\Gamma_2 \vdash \theta$, then $\Gamma_1, \Gamma_2 \vdash \theta'$, where θ' is obtained from θ by replacing one or more occurrences of t_1 with t_2 and/or vice versa.

The rule (=E) indicates a certain restriction in the expressive resources of our language. Suppose, for example, that Sal is identical to Harry (since his mischievous parents gave him two names). According to most people's intuitions, it would not follow from this and "Samantha knows that Sal is bright" that "Samantha knows that Harry is bright," for the reason that Samantha might not know that Sal is the same person as Harry. Contexts like this, in which identicals cannot safely be substituted for each other, are called "opaque." We assume that our language $\mathcal{L}1K$= has no opaque contexts.

One final clause completes the description of the deductive system D:

- (*) That's all folks: $\Gamma \vdash \theta$ only if θ follows from members of Γ by the above rules.

Again, this clause allows proofs by induction on the rules used to establish an argument. If a property of arguments holds of all instances of (As) and (=I), and if the other rules preserve the property, then every argument that is deducible in D enjoys the property in question.

Before moving on to the model theory for $\mathcal{L}1K$=, we pause to note a few features of the deductive system. To illustrate the level of rigor, we begin with a lemma that if a sentence does not contain a particular closed term, we can make some changes to the set of sentences we prove it from without problems. We allow ourselves the liberty here of extending some previous notation: for

---

[8] The rules ($\forall$I) and ($\exists$E) invoke the role of constants denoting individual, but unspecified, objects or persons.

any closed terms t and t', and any sentence θ, we say that $\theta(t|t')$ is the result of replacing all occurrences of t in θ with t'.

Lemma 4.1 *If Γ_1 and Γ_2 differ only in that wherever Γ_1 contains θ, Γ_2 contains $\theta(t|t')$, then for any sentence ϕ not containing t or t', if $\Gamma_1 \vdash \phi$, then $\Gamma_2 \vdash \phi$.*

Proof. The proof proceeds by induction on the number of steps in the proof of ϕ.

Theorem 4.2 (The Rule of Weakening) *If $\Gamma_1 \vdash \phi$ and $\Gamma_1 \subseteq \Gamma_2$, then $\Gamma_2 \vdash \phi$.*

Proof. Again, we proceed by induction on the number of rules that were used to arrive at $\Gamma_1 \vdash \phi$.

Theorem 4.2 allows us to add on premises at will. As we shall see, some alternative systems of logic do not have Weakening. Examples are relevance logic (see Section 9) and some substructural logics (not treated here). This is generally for the same reasons these logicians reject (EFQ): the rule does not seem to fit with our everyday reasoning practices.

By clause (*), all derivations are established in a finite number of steps. So we have

Theorem 4.3 $\Gamma \vdash \phi$ *if and only if there is a finite $\Gamma' \subseteq \Gamma$ such that $\Gamma' \vdash \phi$.*

The next theorem shows that every instance of (EFQ) is provable.

Theorem 4.4 *The rule of ex falso quodlibet is a "derived rule" of D: if $\Gamma_1 \vdash \theta$ and $\Gamma_2 \vdash \neg\theta$, then $\Gamma_1, \Gamma_2 \vdash \psi$, for any sentence ψ.*

The Cut rule is sometimes thought of as essential to a logical system.

Theorem 4.5 (The rule of Cut) *If $\Gamma_1 \vdash \psi$ and $\Gamma_2, \psi \vdash \theta$, then $\Gamma_1, \Gamma_2 \vdash \theta$.*

Proof. Suppose $\Gamma_1 \vdash \psi$ and $\Gamma_2, \psi \vdash \theta$. We proceed by induction on the number of rules used to establish $\Gamma_2, \psi \vdash \theta$. Suppose that n is a natural number, and that the theorem holds for any argument that was derived using fewer than n rules. Suppose that $\Gamma_2, \psi \vdash \theta$ was derived using exactly n rules. If the last rule used was (=I), then $\Gamma_1, \Gamma_2 \vdash \theta$ is also an instance of (=I). If $\Gamma_2, \psi \vdash \theta$ is an instance of (As), then either θ is ψ, or θ is a member of Γ_2. In the former case, we have $\Gamma_1 \vdash \theta$ by supposition, and get $\Gamma_1, \Gamma_2 \vdash \theta$ by Weakening (Theorem 4.2). In the latter case, $\Gamma_1, \Gamma_2 \vdash \theta$ is itself an instance of (As). Suppose that $\Gamma_2, \psi \vdash \theta$ was obtained using ($\wedge$E). Then we have $\Gamma_2, \psi \vdash (\theta \wedge \phi)$. The induction hypothesis gives us $\Gamma_1, \Gamma_2 \vdash (\theta \wedge \phi)$, and ($\wedge$E) produces $\Gamma_1, \Gamma_2 \vdash \theta$. The remaining cases are similar.

Theorem 4.5 allows us to chain together inferences. This fits the practice of establishing theorems and lemmas and then using those theorems and lemmas later at will. The Cut principle is, some think, essential to reasoning. In some logical systems, the Cut principle is a deep theorem; in others it is invalid. The system here was designed, in part, to make the proof of Theorem 4.5 straightforward.

If $\Gamma \vdash \theta$, then we say that the sentence θ is a *deductive consequence* of the set of sentences Γ, and that the argument $\langle \Gamma, \theta \rangle$ is *deductively valid*. A sentence θ is a *logical theorem*, or a *deductive logical truth*, if $\vdash \theta$. That is, θ is a logical theorem if it is a deductive consequence of the empty set. A set Γ of sentences is *consistent* if there is no sentence θ such that $\Gamma \vdash \theta$ and $\Gamma \vdash \neg\theta$. That is, a set is consistent if it does not entail a pair of contradictory opposite sentences.

Theorem 4.6 *A set Γ is consistent if and only if there is a sentence θ such that it is not the case that $\Gamma \vdash \theta$.*

Define a set Γ of sentences of the language $\mathcal{L}1K=$ to be *maximally consistent* if Γ is consistent, and, for every sentence θ of $\mathcal{L}1K=$, if θ is not in Γ, then Γ, θ is inconsistent. In other words, Γ is maximally consistent if Γ is consistent, and adding any sentence in the language not already in Γ renders it inconsistent. It is a straightforward exercise to show that if Γ is maximally consistent then, for any sentence θ, $\Gamma \vdash \theta$ if and only if θ is in Γ.

Theorem 4.7 (The Lindenbaum Lemma) *Let Γ be any consistent set of sentences of $\mathcal{L}1K=$. Then there is a set Γ' of sentences of $\mathcal{L}1K=$ such that $\Gamma \subseteq \Gamma'$ and Γ' is maximally consistent.*

This proof requires the use of a principle corresponding to the law of excluded middle. Intuitionists, who demur from excluded middle, do not accept the Lindenbaum lemma.

5 Model-Theoretic Semantics

Let K be a set of non-logical terminology. An *interpretation* for the language $\mathcal{L}1K =$ is a structure $M = \langle d, I \rangle$, where d is a non-empty set, called the *domain-of-discourse*, or simply the *domain*, of the interpretation, and I is an *interpretation function*. Informally, the domain is what we interpret the language $\mathcal{L}1K=$ to be about: it is what the variables range over. The interpretation function assigns appropriate extensions to the non-logical terms. In particular,

- If c is a constant in K, then $I(c)$ is a member of the domain d. Thus we assume that every constant denotes something. Systems where this is not assumed are called *free logics*. Continuing:

- If f is an n-ary function in K, then $I(f)$ is a function from d^n (the set of all n-tuples of members of d) to d.
- If P^0 is a zero-place predicate letter in K, then $I(P)$ is a truth value, either truth or falsehood.
- If Q^1 is a one-place predicate letter in K, then $I(Q)$ is a subset of d. The idea is that $I(Q)$ is the set of members of the domain that the predicate Q holds of in the interpretation.
- If R^2 is a two-place predicate letter in K, then $I(R)$ is a set of ordered pairs of members of d. Here, $I(R)$ is the set of pairs of members of the domain that the relation R holds between.
- In general, if S^n is an n-place predicate letter in K, then $I(S)$ is a set of ordered n-tuples of members of d.

Define s to be a *variable-assignment*, or simply an *assignment*, on an interpretation M, if s is a function from the variables of the language to the domain d of M. The role of variable-assignments is to assign denotations to the *free* variables of open formulas. In a sense, the quantifiers determine the "meaning" of the bound variables.

For each interpretation M and each variable assignment s under M, we define the *denotation* of each term of the language in M under s. We proceed by recursion:

- If c is a constant, then $D_{M,s}(c)$ is $I(c)$.
- If v is a variable, then $D_{M,s}(v)$ is $s(v)$.
- If f is an n-ary function symbol and $t_1, \ldots t_n$ are terms, then $D_{M,s}(ft_1...t_n)$ is $I(f)(I(t_1)...I(t_n))$.

In sum, the interpretation M assigns denotations to the constants, while the variable-assignment assigns denotations to the (free) variables.

We now define a relation of *satisfaction* between interpretations, variable-assignments, and formulas of $\mathcal{L}1K=$. If ϕ is a formula of $\mathcal{L}1K=$, M is an interpretation for $\mathcal{L}1K=$, and s is a variable-assignment on M, then we write $M, s \vDash \phi$ for M satisfies ϕ under the assignment s. The idea is that $M, s \vDash \phi$ is an analogue of "ϕ comes out true when interpreted as in M via s."

We proceed by recursion on the complexity of the formulas of $\mathcal{L}1K=$:

- If t_1 and t_2 are terms, then $M, s \vDash t_1 = t_2$ if and only if $D_{M,s}(t_1)$ is the same as $D_{M,s}(t_2)$.

This is about as straightforward as it gets. An identity $t_1 = t_2$ comes out true if and only if the terms t_1 and t_2 denote the same thing.

- If P^0 is a zero-place predicate letter in K, then $M, s \vDash P$ if and only if $I(P)$ is truth.
- If S^n is an n-place predicate letter in K and $t_1, \ldots, t_n$ are terms, then $M, s \vDash St_1 \ldots t_n$ if and only if the n-tuple $\langle D_{M,s}(t_1), \ldots, D_{M,s}(t_n) \rangle$ is in $I(S)$.

This takes care of the atomic formulas. We now proceed to the compound formulas of the language, more or less following the meanings of the English counterparts of the logical terminology.

- $M, s \vDash \neg\theta$ if and only if it is not the case that $M, s \vDash \theta$.
- $M, s \vDash (\theta \wedge \psi)$ if and only if both $M, s \vDash \theta$ and $M, s \vDash \psi$.
- $M, s \vDash (\theta \vee \psi)$ if and only if either $M, s \vDash \theta$ or $M, s \vDash \psi$.
- $M, s \vDash (\theta \rightarrow \psi)$ if and only if either it is not the case that $M, s \vDash \theta$, or $M, s \vDash \psi$.
- $M, s \vDash \forall v\theta$ if and only if $M, s' \vDash \theta$, for every assignment s' that agrees with s except possibly at the variable v.

The idea here is that $\forall v\theta$ comes out true if and only if θ comes out true no matter what is assigned to the variable v. The final clause is similar.

- $M, s \vDash \exists v\theta$ if and only if $M, s' \vDash \theta$, for some assignment s' that agrees with s except possibly at the variable v.

So $\exists v\theta$ comes out true if there is an assignment to v that makes θ true.

This semantics is often attributed to Alfred Tarski, and so called a Tarskian semantics. Theorem 3.6, unique readability, assures us that this definition is coherent. At each stage in breaking down a formula, there is exactly one clause to be applied, and so we never get contradictory verdicts concerning satisfaction.

As indicated, the role of variable-assignments is to give denotations to the free variables. We now show that variable-assignments play no other role.

Theorem 5.1 *For any formula θ, if s_1 and s_2 agree on the free variables in θ, then $M, s_1 \vDash \theta$ if and only if $M, s_2 \vDash \theta$.*

Proof. This proof proceeds by induction on the complexity of the formula θ.

By Theorem 5.1, if θ is a sentence, and s_1, s_2, are any two variable-assignments, then $M, s_1 \vDash \theta$ if and only if $M, s_2 \vDash \theta$. So we can just write $M \vDash \theta$ if $M, s \vDash \theta$ for some, or all, variable-assignments s.

Suppose that $K' \subseteq K$ are two sets of non-logical terms. If $M = \langle d, I \rangle$ is an interpretation of $\mathcal{L}1K=$, then we define the *restriction* of M to $\mathcal{L}1K'$ be the interpretation $M' = \langle d, I' \rangle$ such that I' is the restriction of I to K'. That is, M

and M' have the same domain and agree on the non-logical terminology in K'. A straightforward induction establishes the following theorems:

Theorem 5.2 *If M' is the restriction of M to $\mathcal{L}1K'$, then for every sentence θ of $\mathcal{L}1K'$, $M \vDash \theta$ if and only if $M' \vDash \theta$.*

and

Theorem 5.3 *If two interpretations M_1 and M_2 have the same domain and agree on all of the non-logical terminology of a sentence θ, then $M_1 \vDash \theta$ if and only if $M_2 \vDash \theta$.*

In short, the satisfaction of a sentence θ only depends on the domain of discourse and the interpretation of the non-logical terminology in θ.

We say that an argument $\langle \Gamma, \theta \rangle$ is *semantically valid*, or just *valid*, written $\Gamma \vDash \theta$, if for every interpretation M of the language, if $M \vDash \psi$, for every member ψ of Γ, then $M \vDash \theta$. If $\Gamma \vDash \theta$, we also say that θ is a *logical consequence*, or *semantic consequence*, or *model-theoretic consequence* of Γ. The definition corresponds to the informal idea that an argument is valid if it is not possible for its premises to all be true and its conclusion false. Our definition of logical consequence also sanctions the common thesis that a valid argument is truth-preserving – to the extent that satisfaction represents truth. Officially, an argument in $\mathcal{L}1K=$ is valid if its conclusion comes out true under every interpretation of the language in which the premises are true. Validity is the model-theoretic counterpart to deducibility.

A sentence θ is *logically true*, or *valid*, if $M \vDash \theta$, for every interpretation M. A sentence is logically true if and only if the sentence is a consequence of the empty set. If θ is logically true, then for any set Γ of sentences, $\Gamma \vDash \theta$. Logical truth is the model-theoretic counterpart of theoremhood.

A sentence θ is *satisfiable* if there is an interpretation M such that $M \vDash \theta$. That is, θ is satisfiable if there is an interpretation that satisfies it. A set Γ of sentences is satisfiable if there is an interpretation M such that $M \vDash \theta$, for every sentence θ in Γ. If Γ is a set of sentences, and if $M \vDash \theta$ for each sentence θ in Γ, then we say that M is a *model of* Γ. So a set of sentences is satisfiable if it has a model. Satisfiability is the model-theoretic counterpart to consistency.

Notice that $\Gamma \vDash \theta$ if and only if the set $\Gamma, \neg\theta$ is not satisfiable. It follows that if a set Γ is not satisfiable, then, if θ is any sentence, $\Gamma \vDash \theta$. This is a model-theoretic counterpart to *ex falso quodlibet* (see Theorem 4.4). We have the following as an analogue to Theorem 4.6:

Theorem 5.4 *Let Γ be a set of sentences. The following are equivalent: (a) Γ is satisfiable; (b) there is no sentence θ such that both $\Gamma \vDash \theta$ and $\Gamma \vDash \neg\theta$; (c) there is some sentence ψ such that it is not the case that $\Gamma \vDash \psi$.*

6 Meta-theory

We now present some results that relate the deductive notions to their model-theoretic counterparts. The first one is fairly intuitive, if a bit tedious, in the natural deduction framework. We motivated both the various rules of the deductive system D and the various clauses in the definition of satisfaction in terms of the meaning of the English counterparts to the logical terminology (more or less, with the same simplifications in both cases). So one would expect that an argument is deducible, or deductively valid, only if it is semantically valid.

Theorem 6.1 (Soundness) *For any sentence θ and set Γ of sentences, if $\Gamma \vdash_D \theta$, then $\Gamma \vDash \theta$.*

Proof. This proof proceeds by induction on the number of clauses used to establish $\Gamma \vdash \theta$.

Corollary 6.2 *Let Γ be a set of sentences. If Γ is satisfiable, then Γ is consistent.*

Even though the deductive system D and the model-theoretic semantics were developed with the meanings of the logical terminology in mind, one should not automatically expect the converse to soundness (or Corollary 6.2) to hold. For all we know so far, we may not have included enough rules of inference to deduce every valid argument. The converses to soundness and Corollary 6.2 are among the most important and influential results in mathematical logic. We begin with the latter.

Theorem 6.3 (Completeness (Gödel 1930)) *Let Γ be a set of sentences. If Γ is consistent, then Γ is satisfiable.*

Proof. There are many ways to proceed with this proof. One, due to Leon Henkin, essentially builds an interpretation of the language from the language itself, using some of the constants as members of the domain of discourse. One can build these models based on Γ and show that these new models are consistent. Finally, one shows that they make Γ satisfiable.

A converse to Soundness (Theorem 6.1) is a straightforward corollary:

Theorem 6.4 *For any sentence θ and set Γ of sentences, if $\Gamma \vDash \theta$, then $\Gamma \vdash \theta$.*

Our next item is a corollary of Theorem 4.3, Soundness (Theorem 6.1), and Completeness:

Corollary 6.5 (Compactness) *A set Γ of sentences is satisfiable if and only if every finite subset of Γ is satisfiable.*

Soundness and completeness together entail that an argument is deducible if and only if it is valid, and a set of sentences is consistent if and only if it is satisfiable. So we can go back and forth between model-theoretic and proof-theoretic notions, transferring properties of one to the other.

The following is a corollary to the Henkin proof of completeness:

Corollary 6.6 (Löwenheim-Skolem Theorem) *Let Γ be a satisfiable set of sentences of the language $\mathcal{L}1K{=}$. If Γ is either finite or countably infinite (i.e., the size of the natural numbers, usually called $\aleph_0$), then Γ has a model whose domain is countable (i.e., either finite or countably infinite).*

In general, let Γ be a satisfiable set of sentences of $\mathcal{L}1K{=}$, and let κ be the larger of the size of Γ and countably infinite (i.e., $\aleph_0$). Then Γ has a model whose domain is at most size κ.[9]

There is a stronger version of Corollary 6.6. Let $M_1 = \langle d_1, I_1 \rangle$ and $M_2 = \langle d_2, I_2 \rangle$ be interpretations of the language $\mathcal{L}1K{=}$. Define M_1 to be a *submodel* of M_2 if (i) $d_1 \subseteq d_2$, (ii) $I_1(c) = I_2(c)$ for each constant c, (iii) for each function symbol f, $I_1(f)$ is the restriction of $I_2(f)$ to d_1, and (iv) for each relation symbol, I_1 is the restriction of I_2 to d_1. For example, if R is a binary relation letter in K, then, for all a, b in d_1, the pair $\langle a, b \rangle$ is in $I_1(R)$ if and only if $\langle a, b \rangle$ is in $I_2(R)$. Notice that if M_1 is a submodel of M_2, then any variable-assignment on M_1 is also a variable-assignment on M_2.

Say that two interpretations $M_1 = \langle d_1, I_1 \rangle, M_2 = \langle d_2, I_2 \rangle$ are *equivalent* if one of them is a submodel of the other, and for any formula of the language and any variable-assignment s on the submodel, $M_1, s \vDash \theta$ if and only if $M_2, s \vDash \theta$. Notice that if two interpretations are equivalent, then they satisfy the same sentences.[10]

Theorem 6.7 (Downward Löwenheim-Skolem Theorem) *Let $M = \langle d, I \rangle$ be an interpretation of the language $\mathcal{L}1K{=}$. Let d_1 be any subset of d, and let κ be the maximum of the size of K, the size of d_1, and the size of countably infinite (the size of $\aleph_0$). Then there is a submodel $M' = \langle d', I' \rangle$ of M such that (1) d' is not larger than κ, and (2) M and M' are equivalent. In particular, if*

---

[9] For more details on Skolem and these theorems, including the associated paradox, see Dean (forthcoming).

[10] The proof of the downward Löwenheim-Skolem theorem invokes the axiom of choice, and indeed, the theorem is equivalent to the axiom of choice.

the set K of non-logical terminology is either finite or countably infinite, then any interpretation has an equivalent submodel whose domain is either finite or countably infinite.

Another corollary to Compactness (Corollary 6.5) is a kind of opposite of the downward Löwenheim-Skolem theorem:

Theorem 6.8 (Upward Löwenheim-Skolem Theorem)   *Let Γ be any set of sentences of $\mathcal{L}1K =$ such that, for each natural number n, there is an interpretation $M_n = \langle d_n, I_n \rangle$, such that d_n has at least n elements, and M_n satisfies every member of Γ. In other words, Γ is satisfiable and there is no finite upper bound to the size of the interpretations that satisfy every member of Γ. Then for any infinite cardinal κ, there is an interpretation $M = \langle d, I \rangle$, such that the size of d is at least κ and M satisfies every member of Γ. In other words, Γ has arbitrarily large models.*

Combined, the downward and upward Löwenheim-Skolem theorems entail that for any satisfiable set Γ of sentences, if there is no finite bound on the models of Γ, then for any infinite cardinal κ, there is a model of Γ whose domain has size *exactly* κ. Moreover, if M is any interpretation whose domain is infinite, then for any infinite cardinal κ, there is an interpretation M' whose domain has size exactly κ such that M and M' are equivalent.

These results indicate a weakness in the expressive resources of first-order languages like $\mathcal{L}1K=$. No satisfiable set of sentences can guarantee that its models are all countably infinite, nor can any satisfiable set of sentences guarantee that its models are uncountable (of a size larger than the natural numbers, or bigger than $\aleph_0$). So in a sense, first-order languages cannot express the notion of "countably infinite."

Let $M_1 = \langle d_1, I_1 \rangle$ and $M_2 = \langle d_2, I_2 \rangle$ be interpretations of the language $\mathcal{L}1K=$. Then M_1 is said to be *isomorphic* to M_2 if there is a one-to-one function F from d_1 onto d_2 that preserves the structure. In particular, if c is a constant, then $F(I_1(c)) = I_2(c)$; if f is a function symbol, then for each $x \in d_1, F(I_1(f)(x)) = I_2(f)(F(x))$; and if C is an n-place predicate letter, then for each $a_1, \ldots a_n \in I_1, \langle a_1 \ldots a_n \rangle \in I_1(C)$ if and only if $\langle F(a_1) \ldots F(a_n) \rangle \in I_2(C)$.

A straightforward induction shows that if M_1 is isomorphic to M_2, then for any sentence A in the language, A is true in M_1 if and only if A is true in M_2. A set of sentences is said to be *categorical* if all of its models are isomorphic to each other. So a categorical theory has only one model, up to isomorphism.

As noted, it follows from the Löwenheim-Skolem theorems that if a set Γ of sentences has a model with an infinite domain, then Γ has a model of every infinite cardinality. So it has models that are not isomorphic to each other. Thus no theory that has an infinite model is categorical. For example, any first-order theory of arithmetic has models that are not isomorphic to the natural numbers, any first-order theory of real analysis has models that are not isomorphic to the real numbers, etc.

Let A be any set of sentences in a first-order language $\mathcal{L}1K=$, where K includes terminology for arithmetic, and assume that every member of A is true of the natural numbers. We can even let A be the set of all sentences in $\mathcal{L}1K=$ that are true of the natural numbers. Then A has uncountable models, indeed models of any infinite cardinality. Such interpretations are among those that are sometimes called *unintended*, or *non-standard*, models of arithmetic. Let B be any set of first-order sentences that are true of the real numbers, and let C be any first-order axiomatization of set theory. Then if B and C are satisfiable (in infinite interpretations), then each of them has countably infinite models. That is, any first-order, satisfiable set theory or theory of the real numbers has (unintended) models the size of the natural numbers. This is despite the fact that a sentence (seemingly) stating that the universe is uncountable is provable in most set theories. This situation, known as the *Skolem paradox*, has generated much discussion (see, e.g., the papers reprinted in Shapiro (1996)). In Section 7, we will look at Higher-order classical logic. Higher-order logics are able to produce models of the theory of real numbers, for example, which do not have unintended models the same size as the naturals. Similarly, higher-order logics can model the theory of the natural numbers without producing any non-standard models.

ALTERNATIVES TO CLASSICAL FIRST-ORDER LOGIC
7 Classical Higher-Order Logic

The formal languages $\mathcal{L}1K$ and $\mathcal{L}1K=$ sketched above only have one sort of variable. These are sometimes called *first-order* variables. Each interpretation of the language has a domain, which is the range of the first-order variables. It is what the language is about, according to the given interpretation. *Second-order* variables range over properties, classes, relations, or functions of the items in that domain. Third-order variables range over properties, or relations, or functions on the items in the range of the second-order variables. Fourth-order variables range over properties, classes, relations, or functions on the items in the range of the third-order variables, etc.

A formal language is *first-order* if it contains first-order variables, and no others. So the languages sketched above are all first-order. A language is *second-order* if it contains first-order and second-order variables, and no others. And on it goes. A language is *higher-order* if it is at least second-order.

Second-order logic is the logic of second-order languages, and *higher-order logic* is the logic of higher-order languages.

It is not an exaggeration to say that first-order logic is the paradigm of contemporary logical theory. The vast majority of the works in both philosophical and mathematical logic concern first-order languages exclusively. Most textbooks do not mention higher-order logic at all, and most of the rest give it scant treatment.

In contrast, almost all of the central work that launched contemporary logic concerns higher-order formal languages. Examples include Frege (1879), Peano (1889), and Whitehead and Russell (1910). First-order logic appeared as a distinctive study only when some authors, beginning with Löwenheim (1915), separated out first-order languages as subsystems for special treatment. Early twentieth-century logicians often referred to the deductive system of first-order logic as the *restricted functional calculus*. For more on the historical emergence of first-order logic, see Moore (1980), Moore (1988), Shapiro (1991, Chapter 7), and Eklund (1996).

7.1 Languages

As above (Section 3.1), let K be a set of non-logical terminology – constants, predicate and relation symbols, and function symbols. Recall our language $\mathcal{L}1K$. The language $\mathcal{L}2K$ is obtained by adding a stock of (second-order) relation variables and function variables. Relation variables are upper-case Roman letters from the end of the alphabet, with or without numerical subscripts. Function variables are letters like f, g, and h, with or without numerical subscripts. We will sometimes use a superscript to indicate the degree, or number of places, of each second-order variable: X^1 is a monadic predicate variable; f^2 is a binary function variable, etc. In most cases, context will suffice to determine the degree.

There are four new formation rules:[11]

- If f^n is an n-place function variable and $t_1, \ldots, t_n$ are terms, then $f^n t_1 \ldots t_n$ is a term.
- If R^n is an n-place relation variable and $t_1, \ldots, t_n$ are terms, then $R^n t_1 \ldots t_n$ is an atomic formula.
- If ϕ is a formula and V a relation variable, then $\forall V \phi$ and $\exists V \phi$ are formulas.
- If ϕ is a formula and f a function variable, then $\forall f \phi$ and $\exists f \phi$ are formulas.

---

[11] We do not mark distinctions between variables in the object language and meta-variables that range over items in the object language. Context will indicate which is meant.

As in the case of first-order languages, a *sentence* is a formula with no free variables. For example, $\exists X \forall x \neg Xx$ asserts the existence of a property that applies to no objects, and has no free variables.

A symbol for identity (between objects in the domain) is introduced as an abbreviation,

$$t = u \leftrightarrow_{df} \forall X(Xt \leftrightarrow Xu)$$

where t and u are terms. The underlying idea is that two objects are identical if they have the same properties, or if they are in the same sets... This is not meant as a deep philosophical thesis concerning the nature of identity (although it is a formalization of the Leibniz Law of the indiscernibility of identicals). If desired, one can drop this and add a primitive, logical identity symbol, as in $\mathcal{L}1K=$.

Sets and classes are *extensional*, in the sense that if A and B are classes with exactly the same members, then A is identical to B. Properties and relations are *intensional*, not extensional, in the sense that there can be two distinct properties that apply to exactly the same things. The property of being a creature with a heart and the property of being a creature with kidneys are sometimes cited as an example of the intensionality of properties, since they apply to the same things, but are different properties.

We do not include a symbol for identity between second-order items, like relations and functions in our formal languages here. This allows us to forestall issues concerning the nature and individuation of these items. One can think of the higher-order items as intensional or one can think of them as extensional, at least as far as the formalism goes. For the most part, we will use words like "property," "class," and "set" interchangeably.

One can expand the set K to include so-called higher-order non-logical constants, terms that stand for things like properties (or sets) of properties, or functions on properties. An example would be a property TWO of properties such that TWO(P) holds just in case P applies to exactly two things.

A third-order language $\mathcal{L}3K$ can be defined from $\mathcal{L}2K$ by adding third-order variables for relations on relations, functions of predicates, functions of functions, etc. Then one could add non-logical constants (to K) for relations on functions of predicates, and the like. Then one could add fourth-order variables ranging over such things, thus producing a fourth-order language, $\mathcal{L}4K$, and so on. No new conceptual issues arise, and we stick to second-order languages here.

7.2 Deductive System

We assume that the set K of non-logical terminology includes infinitely many constants, predicate, and function symbols of each degree. The introduction and elimination rules for negation and the binary connectives are the same as in Section 4. Let Θ be a formula, V a predicate variable, and B a non-logical predicate with the same number of places. Then let $\Theta(V|B)$ be the result of substituting B for each free occurrence of V in Θ. Similarly, if h is a function variable and d a non-logical function symbol with the same number of places, then $\Theta(h|d)$ is the result of substituting d for each free occurrence of h in Θ.

The introduction and elimination rules for the second-order quantifiers are direct analogues of those for the first-order quantifiers. Let Γ, Γ_1, and Γ_2 be sets of sentences and ϕ, ψ sentences:

- ($\forall$E):
  If $\Gamma \vdash \forall V\phi$, then $\Gamma \vdash \phi(V|B)$.
  If $\Gamma \vdash \forall h\phi$, then $\Gamma \vdash \phi(h|d)$.
- ($\forall$I):
  If $\Gamma \vdash \phi(V|B)$, then $\Gamma \vdash \forall V\phi$, provided that B does not occur anywhere in Γ or in ϕ.
  If $\Gamma \vdash \phi(h|d)$, then $\Gamma \vdash \forall h\phi$, provided that d does not occur anywhere in Γ or in ϕ.
- ($\exists$I):
  If $\Gamma \vdash \phi(V|B)$, then $\Gamma \vdash \exists V\phi$.
  If $\Gamma \vdash \phi(h|d)$, then $\Gamma \vdash \exists h\phi$.
- ($\exists$E):
  If $\Gamma_1 \vdash \exists V\phi$ and $\Gamma_2, \phi(V|B) \vdash \psi$, then $\Gamma_1, \Gamma_2 \vdash \psi$, provided that V does not occur in ϕ, Γ_2, or ψ.
  If $\Gamma_1 \vdash \exists h\phi$ and $\Gamma_2, \phi(h|d) \vdash \psi$, then $\Gamma_1, \Gamma_2 \vdash \psi$, provided that d does not occur in ϕ, Γ_2, or ψ.

So, as in the first-order case, higher-order terms can play the role of parameters or free variables.

The next item is a *comprehension scheme*. Let ϕ be a formula whose free variables are among $x_1, \ldots x_n$, and let V be an n-place relation variable that does not occur in ϕ. Then the following is an axiom – it can be asserted at any time in a derivation:

$$\exists X \forall x_1 \ldots \forall x_n (Xx_1 \ldots x_n \leftrightarrow \phi(x_1, \ldots x_n)).$$

Taken together, the instances of the comprehension scheme register the thesis that every formula determines a relation or, more precisely, for every formula there is a relation that holds of the same objects or n-tuples.

If the embedded formula ϕ contains bound second-order variables, then the corresponding instance of comprehension is called *impredicative*. In effect, we define a relation using a bound variable ranging over all relations (including the one defined). Some authors do not allow impredicative instances of comprehension. Bertrand Russell (1908, p. 237), for example, argues that such "definitions" are circular; they run afoul of the *Vicious Circle Principle*:

> No totality can contain members defined in terms of itself.

Or Russell (1973, p. 198):

> Whatever in any way concerns all or any or some of a class must not be itself one of the members of a class.

See Feferman (2006) for an account of how the restrictions might be implemented. Here, we adopt the full, impredicative comprehension scheme.

Recall that identity (on the first-order terms) is defined:

$$t = u \leftrightarrow_{df} \forall X(Xt \leftrightarrow Xu).$$

One can show that the rules for identity in first-order systems can be derived here (assuming full comprehension). The introduction rule (=I) is: $\Gamma \vdash t = t$. By our definition, that is

$$\forall X(Xt \leftrightarrow Xt).$$

It is an easy exercise to derive this sentence from no undischarged premises.

The elimination rule (=E) is: if $\Gamma_1 \vdash t = u$ and $\Gamma_2 \vdash \phi$ then $\Gamma_1, \Gamma_2 \vdash \phi'$, where ϕ' is obtained from ϕ by replacing some occurrences of t with u. So suppose that $\Gamma_1 \vdash t = u$, i.e., $\Gamma_1 \vdash \forall X(Xt \leftrightarrow Xu)$. And suppose $\Gamma_2 \vdash \phi$. Let ψ be the result of replacing the occurrences of t in ϕ that are themselves replaced with u in ϕ' with a variable x that does not otherwise occur in ϕ. Notice that $\psi(x|t)$ is just ϕ, and $\psi(x|u)$ is ϕ'.

The following is an instance of comprehension:

$$\exists X \forall x(Xx \leftrightarrow \psi(x)).$$

Let C be a predicate letter that does not occur in Γ_1, Γ_2 or ϕ, and let Γ_3 contain only the following:

$$\forall x(Cx \leftrightarrow \psi(x)).$$

We have $\Gamma_1, \Gamma_2 \vdash \phi$, which is $\Gamma_1, \Gamma_2 \vdash \psi(x|t)$. So $\Gamma_1, \Gamma_2, \Gamma_3 \vdash Ct$. So $\Gamma_1, \Gamma_2, \Gamma_3 \vdash Cu$ (since $\Gamma_1 \vdash Ct \leftrightarrow Cu$). We thus have $\Gamma_1, \Gamma_2, \Gamma_3 \vdash \psi(x|u)$. But this is $\Gamma_1, \Gamma_2, \Gamma_3 \vdash \phi'$. So $\Gamma_1, \Gamma_2 \vdash \phi'$, by an application of the elimination rule for the second-order existential quantifier (in light of the above instance of comprehension).

The final item in the deductive system is a version of the *axiom of choice*. Let X be an $n+1$-place relation variable and f an n-place function variable. Then the following is an axiom:

$$\forall X(\forall x_1 \ldots \forall x_n \exists y X x_1 \ldots x_n y \rightarrow \exists f \forall x_1 \ldots \forall x_n X x_1 \ldots x_n f x_1 \ldots x_n).$$

The antecedent of this conditional asserts that, for each sequence $x_1, \ldots, x_n$ there is at least one y such that the sequence $x_1, \ldots, x_n, y$ satisfies X. The consequent asserts the existence of a function that "picks out" one such y for each $x_1, \ldots, x_n$.

The axiom of choice has a long and at least once-controversial history (see Moore (1982)). If the reader has qualms about the axiom of choice, or about calling the axiom of choice a principle of logic, it can be dropped from the system. If this reader wishes to retain functions, she can add a comprehension principle that relates functions to appropriate relations:

$$\forall X(\forall x_1 \ldots \forall x_n \exists y \forall z(X x_1 \ldots x_n z \leftrightarrow z = y) \rightarrow \exists f \forall x_1 \ldots \forall x_n X x_1 \ldots x_n f x_1 \ldots x_n).$$

The antecedent of the embedded conditional asserts that, for each sequence $x_1, \ldots x_n$, there is *exactly one* y such that the sequence $x_1, \ldots x_n, y$ satisfies X. The consequent asserts the existence of a corresponding function. This sentence follows from the above axiom of choice.

Call our deductive system D2.

7.3 Model Theory

Recall that, for first-order languages, an *interpretation* is a structure $M = \langle d, I \rangle$, where is d a non-empty set, called the *domain-of-discourse*, or simply the *domain*, of the interpretation, and I is an interpretation function. Informally, the domain is what we interpret the language to be about. It is what the (first-order) variables range over. The interpretation function assigns appropriate extensions to the non-logical terminology.

For a given interpretation, a *variable-assignment* is a function from the (first-order) variables to the domain. For each interpretation and variable-assignment, there is a denotation function that assigns a member of the domain to each term. We then defined a relation of *satisfaction* between formulas, interpretations, and variable-assignments. Then the various logical notions, such as validity, were defined in terms of satisfaction.

This section presents three model-theoretic semantics for the second-order languages $\mathcal{L}2K$, and provides a brief sketch of a fourth. Each of them builds on the model theory for the corresponding first-order language, in the sense that each interpretation has, as components, a domain d and an interpretation function *I*, as in Section 5. We add a range for the relation and function variables, and then show how the denotation function and the satisfaction relation apply to the new terms and the new atomic formulas, respectively. The rest is straightforward.

7.3.1 Standard Semantics

The name "standard" here is more or less common among writers on this topic. Critics sometimes put the word "standard" in scare quotes, or use phrases like "so-called 'standard' semantics." In a sense to be made clear below, it is only standard semantics that makes the logic distinctively second-order.

A *standard interpretation* of $\mathcal{L}2K$ is the same as an interpretation of the corresponding first-order language, namely, a structure $\langle d, I \rangle$. The range of the *n*-place relation variables is the entire powerset of d^n, the class of all sets of *n*-tuples of members of *d*. Similarly, the range of the *n*-place function variables is the class of all functions from d^n to *d*. So a variable-assignment on an interpretation is a function that assigns a member of the domain *d* to each first-order variable, a subset of d^n to each *n*-place relation variable, and a function from d^n to *d* to each *n*-place function variable.

To belabor the obvious, function variables are assigned to functions. So the denotation function for the terms of $\mathcal{L}2K$ is a straightforward extension of the denotation function from the corresponding first-order language. The new clause is:

- Let $M = \langle d, I \rangle$ be an interpretation and *s* a variable-assignment on *M*. If *f* is an *n*-place function variable and $t_1, \ldots t_n$ are terms, the denotation of $ft_1, \ldots t_n$ is the result of applying the function $s(f)$ assigned to *f* to the denotations of the terms $t_1, \ldots t_n$.

The clause for the satisfaction of the new atomic formulas is:

- Let $M = \langle d, I \rangle$ be an interpretation *s* a variable-assignment on M. If *X* is an *n*-place relation variable and $t_1, \ldots t_n$ are terms, then $M, s \vDash Xt_1, \ldots t_n$ if and only if the sequence consisting of the denotations of the terms $t_1, \ldots t_n$ is a member of $s(X)$.

The connectives and first-order quantifiers are interpreted as in the first-order case. The clauses for the new quantifiers are the straightforward analogue of the clauses for the first-order quantifiers:

- $M, s \vDash \forall X\phi$ if and only if $M, s' \vDash \phi$, for every variable assignment s' that agrees with *s* at every variable except possibly *X*.

- $M, s \vDash \exists X\phi$ if and only if $M, s' \vDash \phi$, for some variable assignment s' that agrees with s at every variable except possibly X.
- $M, s \vDash \forall f\phi$ if and only if $M, s' \vDash \phi$, for every variable assignment s' that agrees with s at every variable except possibly f.
- $M, s \vDash \exists f\phi$ if and only if $M, s' \vDash \phi$, for some variable assignment s' that agrees with s at every variable except possibly f.

As in the first-order case, if our formula ϕ is a sentence, then the variable assignment does no work. We can speak directly of whether $M \vDash \phi$.

The logical notions all carry over, word for word:

- A sentence ϕ of $\mathcal{L}2K$ is a *standard logical truth* if and only if $M \vDash \phi$, for every standard interpretation M.
- A set Γ of sentences of $\mathcal{L}2K$ is *standardly satisfiable* if and only if there is an interpretation M such that $M \vDash \psi$ for every $\psi \in \Gamma$.
- A sentence ϕ of $\mathcal{L}2K$ is a *standard consequence* of a set Γ of sentences of $\mathcal{L}2K$, written $\Gamma \vDash_s \phi$ if, and only if, for every interpretation M, if $M \vDash \psi$, for every $\psi \in \Gamma$, then $M \vDash \phi$.

Again, a standard interpretation for $\mathcal{L}2K$ is the same as an interpretation for its first-order counterpart $\mathcal{L}1K$ (or $\mathcal{L}1K=$), namely, a domain and an interpretation of the non-logical terminology. That is, in standard semantics, by fixing a domain one thereby fixes the range of both the first-order variables and the second-order variables. There is no further "interpreting" to be done.

This is not the case for the next two model-theoretic frameworks introduced in this section. In those cases, one separately determines a range for the first-order variables and ranges for the second-order variables.

7.3.2 Henkin Semantics

The central feature of *Henkin semantics* is that in a given interpretation, the relation variables range over a *fixed collection* of relations on the domain, which may not include all of the relations; the function variables range over a fixed collection of functions on the domain, which may not contain all of the functions. A *Henkin interpretation* $\mathcal{L}2K$ is a structure $M^H = \langle d, D, F, I \rangle$, in which d is a domain and I an interpretation function for the non-logical terminology, as above.

The new items are sequences. For each n, $D(n)$ is a non-empty subset of the powerset of d^n and $F(n)$ is a non-empty set of functions from d^n to d. The idea is that $D(n)$ is the range of the n-place relation variables and $F(n)$ is the range of the n-place function variables.

A *variable-assignment* on M^H is a function that assigns a member of d to each first-order variable, a member of $D(n)$ to each n-place relation variable, and a member of $F(n)$ to each n-place function variable.

The rest of the presentation of this semantics is the same as that of standard semantics, almost word for word. The clause for denotation is:

- Let $M^H = \langle d, D, F, I \rangle$ be a Henkin interpretation and s a variable-assignment on M^H. If f is an n-place function variable and $t_1, \ldots t_n$ are terms, the denotation of $ft_1, \ldots t_n$ is the result of applying the function $s(f)$ assigned to f to the denotations of the terms $t_1, \ldots t_n$.

The clause for the satisfaction of the new atomic formulas is:

- Let $M^H = \langle d, D, F, I \rangle$ be a Henkin interpretation and s a variable-assignment on M^H. If X is an n-place relation variable and $t_1, \ldots t_n$ are terms, then $M^H, s \vDash Xt_1, \ldots t_n$ if and only if the sequence consisting of the denotations of the terms $t_1, \ldots t_n$ is a member of $s(X)$.

The clauses for the second-order quantifiers are:

- $M^H, s \vDash \forall X\phi$ if and only if $M^H, s' \vDash \phi$, for every variable assignment s' that agrees with s at every variable except possibly X.
- $M^H, s \vDash \exists X\phi$ if and only if $M^H, s' \vDash \phi$, for some variable assignment s' that agrees with s at every variable except possibly X.
- $M^H, s \vDash \forall f\phi$ if and only if $M^H, s' \vDash \phi$, for every variable assignment s' that agrees with s at every variable except possibly f.
- $M^H, s \vDash \exists f\phi$ if and only if $M^H, s' \vDash \phi$, for some variable assignment s' that agrees with s at every variable except possibly f.

In these four clauses, what distinguishes standard from Henkin semantics is the range of the phrases "every variable assignment" and "some variable assignment." In a Henkin interpretation, we only consider the functions that assign members of the various $D(n)$ and $F(n)$ to the second-order variables, while in standard semantics, we consider every such function.

The logical notions also carry over in a straightforward manner:

- A sentence ϕ of $\mathcal{L}2K$ is a *Henkin logical truth* if and only if $M^H \vDash \phi$, for every Henkin interpretation M^H.
- A set Γ of sentences of $\mathcal{L}2K$ is *Henkin satisfiable* if and only if there is a Henkin interpretation M^H such that $M^H \vDash \psi$ for every $\psi \in \Gamma$.
- A sentence ϕ of $\mathcal{L}2K$ is a *Henkin consequence* of a set Γ of sentences of $\mathcal{L}2K$, written $\Gamma \vDash_H \phi$ if and only if, for every Henkin interpretation M^H, if $M^H \vDash \psi$, for every $\psi \in \Gamma$, then $M^H \vDash \phi$.

There is a sense in which a standard interpretation of $\mathcal{L}2K$ is equivalent to the Henkin interpretation in which, for each n, $D(n)$ is the entire powerset of d^n, and $F(n)$ is the collection of all functions from d^n to d. Such Henkin interpretations are sometimes called *full interpretations*.

The equivalence can be made precise. Let M be a standard interpretation and let M^F be the corresponding full Henkin interpretation. Then for each assignment s and each formula ϕ, $M, s \vDash \phi$ if and only if $M^F, s \vDash \phi$. In effect, standard semantics just is the restriction of Henkin semantics to full interpretations.

Notice that on both standard semantics and Henkin semantics, the items in the range of second-order variables are extensional entities – either sets or functions. Recall, however, that there is no symbol for "higher-order identity" in the language. As noted, one is free to maintain an intensional understanding of the higher-order entities, and think of them as attributes, properties, or propositional functions. For the purposes of model-theoretic semantics, sets can serve as surrogates for the relevant intensional items. If an advocate of intensional items believes that for every arbitrary collection S of n-tuples on the domain, there is a property whose extension is S, then she will favor standard semantics. Otherwise, we presume that the advocate would favor Henkin semantics (see Cocchiarella (1988)).

7.3.3 Multi-sorted, First-order Semantics

Here we drop the assumption that the items in the range of the second-order variables are extensional entities, like sets or functions. A *first-order interpretation* of $\mathcal{L}2K$ is a structure $M^1 = \langle d, d_1, d_2, \langle I, p, a \rangle \rangle$, in which d is a non-empty set and I an interpretation function assigning items constructed from d to the items in K, as above. For each natural number n, $d_1(n)$ and $d_2(n)$ are non-empty sets. They are the ranges of the n-place relation variables and the n-place function variables, respectively. For each n, $p(n)$ is a subset of $d^n \times d_1(n)$. This represents the interpretation of the "predication" relation in M^1, between an n-place "relation" R in M^1 and n-tuples from the domain, those that have the relation. It is a sort of meta-relation, or a meta-theoretic relation. For example, suppose that $d_1(1)$ has an object D. This would represent a property or a set. Then $\langle c, D \rangle$ would be a member of $p(1)$ if and only if c is supposed to have that property or be a member of that set. In like manner, for each natural number n, $a(n)$ is a function from $d^n \times d_2(n)$ to d. Here, $a(n)$ is the interpretation of the n-place "application" function in M^1, from the collection of sequences and the "functions" in M^1 to the first domain.

The rest is fairly straightforward, if a bit tedious. A *variable-assignment* on M^1 is a function that assigns a member of d to each first-order variable, a member of $d_1(n)$ to each n-place relation variable, and a member of $d_2(n)$ to each n-place function variable. The relevant clause for denotation is:

- Let M^1 be a first-order interpretation and s an assignment on M^1. If f is an n-place function variable and $t_1, \ldots t_n$ are terms, then the denotation of $ft_1 \ldots t_n$ is the result of applying $a(n)$ to the denotations of $t_1, \ldots, t_n$ and $s(f)$.

In other words, the denotation of $ft_1 \ldots t_n$ is determined by the "application" function $a(n)$, evaluated at the denotations of the items in $t_1, \ldots, t_n$ and the item in $d_2(n)$ assigned to f by s.

The clause for the satisfaction of atomic formulas is similar:

- Let M^1 be a first-order interpretation and s a variable assignment on M^1. If X is an n-place relation variable and $t_1, \ldots, t_n$ are terms, then $M^1, s \vDash Xt_1 \ldots t_n$ if and only if the sequence consisting of the denotations of $t_1, \ldots, t_n$ and $s(X)$ is a member of $p(n)$.

Here, the atomic formula is interpreted via the "predication" relation $p(n)$.

The clauses for the quantifiers then carry over:

- $M^1, s \vDash \forall X\phi$ if and only if $M^1, s' \vDash \phi$, for every variable assignment s' that agrees with s at every variable except possibly X.
- $M^1, s \vDash \exists X\phi$ if and only if $M^1, s' \vDash \phi$, for some variable assignment s' that agrees with s at every variable except possibly X.
- $M^1, s \vDash \forall f\phi$ if and only if $M^1, s' \vDash \phi$, for every variable assignment s' that agrees with s at every variable except possibly f.
- $M^1, s \vDash \exists f\phi$ if and only if $M^1, s' \vDash \phi$, for some variable assignment s' that agrees with s at every variable except possibly f.

And the logical notions:

- A sentence ϕ of $\mathcal{L}2K$ is a *first-order logical truth* if and only if $M^1 \vDash \phi$, for every first-order interpretation M^1.
- A set Γ of sentences of $\mathcal{L}2K$ is *first-order satisfiable* if and only if there is a first-order interpretation M^1 such that $M^1 \vDash \psi$ for every $\psi \in \Gamma$.
- A sentence ϕ of $\mathcal{L}2K$ is a $\widehat{\text{first}}$-order consequence of a set Γ of sentences of $\mathcal{L}2K$, written $\Gamma \vDash_1 \phi$ if and only if for every first-order interpretation M^1, if $M^1 \vDash \psi$, for every $\psi \in \Gamma$, then $M^1 \vDash \phi$.

Notice that a given Henkin interpretation $\langle d, D, F, I \rangle$ is equivalent to the first-order interpretation $\langle d, d_1, d_2, \langle I, p, a \rangle \rangle$ in which d_1 is D, d_2 is F, p recapitulates the "real" predication (or membership) relation between d and the various $D(n)$, and a recapitulates the "real" application function from d^n and the various $F(n)$ to d. That is, for each n, $\langle u, v \rangle$ is in $p(n)$ if and only if $u \in v$; and

$a(n)(u, w) = w(u)$. Thus, for every Henkin interpretation M^H there is a first-order interpretation M^1, such that for every assignment s on M^H there is an assignment s^1 on M^1, such that for every formula ϕ of $\mathcal{L}2K$, $M^H, s \vDash \phi$ if and only if $M^1, s^1 \vDash \phi$.

There is a converse as well. Let $M^1 = \langle d, d_1, d_2, \langle I, p, a \rangle \rangle$ be a first-order interpretation of $\mathcal{L}2K$. Then there is a Henkin interpretation $M^H = \langle d, D, F, I \rangle$ such that for every variable-assignment s on M^1 there is an assignment s^H on M^H, such that for every formula ϕ of $\mathcal{L}2K, M^1, s \vDash \phi$ if and only if $M^H, s^H \vDash \phi$ (see Shapiro (1991, Chapter 3) for details). The idea is that we replace an item c of, say, $d_1(2)$ with the set of pairs of elements of d that c "holds of," according to $p(2)$. To take a frivolous example, suppose that in M^1, d is a set of grapes and $d_1(2)$ is a set of tomatoes. Then in the corresponding M^H, each tomato is "replaced" by the set of pairs of grapes that bear the M^1-interpretation of the predication relation to it.

It follows that, for each sentence ϕ of $\mathcal{L}2K$, ϕ is a Henkin logical truth if and only if ϕ is a first-order logical truth; for each set Γ of sentences, Γ is Henkin-satisfiable if and only if Γ is first-order-satisfiable; and ϕ is a Henkin-consequence of Γ if and only if ϕ is a first-order-consequence of Γ. In short, Henkin semantics and first-order semantics are pretty much the same.[12]

7.3.4 Plural Quantification

All three of the above model-theoretic semantics follow the prevailing custom of assigning each variable to a distinctive *range* in each interpretation, and in each case, the range is a *set*. On standard, Henkin, and first-order semantics, the range of each first-order variable is a (non-empty) set, and the range of a given higher-order variable is a set of sets (of n-tuples) or a set of functions. So all three semantics preclude an interpretation of a language like $\mathcal{L}2K$ in which the first-order variables do not range over a set. So we cannot give an account of set theory in which the intended first-order variables range over every member of the iterative hierarchy, for the reason that typical set theories, such as that of Zermelo-Fraenkel, entail that there is no set of all sets. So if we are to have a higher-order set theory, what would its higher-order variables range over?

In response to issues like these, George Boolos (1984; 1985) proposed a different way to understand at least monadic, second-order relation variables. According to both standard and Henkin semantics, an existential quantifier $\exists X$ should be read "there is a set X" or "there is a property X," in which case, of

---

[12] See Shapiro (1991, Chapter 3) and Gilmore (1957). This equivalence is due to our decision to not introduce an identity relation on the higher-order items. Thanks to a referee for highlighting this.

course, the locution invokes sets or properties. Against this, Boolos suggests that a monadic, second-order quantifier be considered a counterpart of a plural quantifier, "there are (objects)."

The following sentence:

Some critics admire only one another

has a (more or less) straightforward second-order rendering:

$$\exists X(\exists xXx \land \forall x \forall y((Xx \land Axy) \rightarrow (x \neq y \land Xy))).$$

According to standard, Henkin, or first-order semantics, this sentence would correspond to "there is a non-empty set C (of critics) such that, for any $x \in C$, and any y, if x admires y, then $x \neq y$ and $y \in C$." In the language of the semantics, however, this reading implies the existence of a set, while the original sentence, "some critics admire only one another," does not, or so it seems.

There is no doubt that native speakers of ordinary natural languages have no trouble with sentences that contain plural quantifiers. Boolos argues that logicians can use plural locutions in the meta-language in which we develop formal, model-theoretic semantics. The plural locution interprets the monadic, second-order quantifier.[13]

So construed, a monadic second-order language does not invoke any ontology beyond that of its first-order counterpart. In a sense, the range of monadic, second-order variables is the same as the range of the first-order variables. It is just that the quantification is plural.

In a second-order formulation of set theory, the "Russell sentence," $\exists X \forall x (Xx \leftrightarrow x \notin x)$, is a consequence of the comprehension scheme. According to standard semantics, Henkin semantics, and first-order semantics, it entails that there is a set whose members are all and only the sets that do not contain themselves. This is easily seen to be contradictory. Is this "Russell set" a member of itself or not? On Boolos's interpretation, the Russell sentence reads, "there are some sets such that any set is one of them just in case it is not a member of itself," a harmless truism. We forgo details of Boolos's (1985)

---

[13] There is an irony here. Godehard Link (1998, p. 314) notes that:

> Boolos sought [an] … interpretation of (monadic) second-order logic … in which the second-order variables are not taken to range over any set-like "collections" of objects from the first-order domain. He found that interpretation in the device of plural quantification in English. Thus a remarkable inversion of the common practice of interpretation and regimentation … [R]ather than explicating natural language in terms of a formal language, a formal language is interpreted in terms of certain natural language locutions.

rigorous, model-theoretic semantics for second-order languages with monadic relation variables.[14]

It seems that the Boolos interpretation for monadic, second-order languages is intended to be equivalent to standard semantics, at least for interpretations in which the domain constitutes a set. We have some doubts as to whether our independent or pre-theoretic grasp of plural quantifiers is sufficiently determinate for this.

Consider a statement of second-order real analysis of the form:

$$\forall X \exists Y \phi(X, Y).$$

The opening second-order quantifiers can be given both a plural and an ordinary, standard reading.[15] It had better be the case that if we read the quantifiers as plurals, we will get exactly the same truth value, in general, as we would if we understand the quantifiers as ranging over sets of real numbers.

In effect, there needs to be a "plurality" (so to speak) for each set of real numbers. Does the English plural construction have that determinate a meaning? To be sure, an advocate of the Boolos plural interpretation can stipulate that she intends the quantifier to have such a meaning in cases like that of real analysis. Notice, however, that one needs some set theory to do this stipulating. This consideration might sustain the complaint of Michael Resnik (1988) and Shapiro (1993) that the sophisticated understanding of the plural construction used in justifying second-order logic is mediated by set theory.

7.4 Meta-theory

Here we provide brief sketches of some of the main meta-theoretic properties of second-order languages, using three of the model-theoretic frameworks (we do not discuss plural quantification). The results vary considerably, depending on which model-theoretric framework is considered. For more detail, see Shapiro (1991, Chapters 4 and 5).

7.4.1 Henkin and First-order Semantics

Since, as noted in the previous section, Henkin semantics is equivalent to first-order semantics for the languages $\mathcal{L}2K$, we need only present the relevant

---

[14] See Linnebo (2017) for an excellent overview of the use of plural quantification in formal contexts.

[15] Let's look at an example. Let $\phi(X, Y)$ be a statement that for all x, Yx holds if and only if x is a limit point of the numbers of which X holds. On a standard reading, $\forall X \exists Y \phi(X, Y)$ says that for every set X there is a set Y that contains all and only the limit points of X (i.e., Y is the closure of X). On a plural reading, the sentence says that for any numbers, there are some numbers such that a number is one of them just in case it is a limit point of the given numbers.

results for whichever of these is more convenient. Anything said about one of them applies directly to the other.

The deductive system D2 is *not* sound for Henkin and first-order semantics. It is straightforward to verify that every Henkin interpretation satisfies the axioms and rules of a first-order deductive system and the introduction and elimination rules for the second-order quantifiers, but some Henkin interpretations do not satisfy instances of the comprehension scheme and some do not satisfy the axiom of choice. Consider, for example, a structure $M^H = \langle d, D, F, I \rangle$ in which the first-order domain d has two distinct members a, b; $D(2)$ has a single member, the relation $\{\langle a, a \rangle, \langle b, a \rangle\}$. Then M^H does not satisfy the following instance of the comprehension scheme:

$$\exists X \forall x \forall y (Xxy \leftrightarrow x = y).$$

In effect, this axiom asserts the existence of the identity relation, but M^H does not contain such a relation.

Define a Henkin (or first-order) interpretation to be *faithful to* D2, or simply *faithful*, if it satisfies every instance of the comprehension scheme (and the axiom of choice if that is included in the deductive system). That is, a Henkin interpretation is faithful if it contains every relation definable via the comprehension scheme (and the functions promised by the axiom of choice). To be sure, there are some faithful interpretations. Recall that a Henkin interpretation is "full" if it contains every set of n-tuples of members of the domain and every function on the domain. So faithful interpretations contain every definable set and every definable function, and so full interpretations are faithful.

All subsequent discussion is restricted to faithful interpretations. Of course, we now have soundness-by-fiat. We just restrict ourselves to Henkin and first-order interpretations that satisfy the axioms and rules of D2.

Languages like $\mathcal{L}2K$ under Henkin semantics and first-order semantics have the meta-theoretic features of ordinary, first-order languages. First, the deductive system D2 is complete for Henkin semantics: Let Γ be a set of sentences and ϕ a sentence of $\mathcal{L}2K$. Then if ϕ is true in every faithful Henkin interpretation of Γ, then ϕ can be deduced from Γ in D2.

The downward Löwenheim-Skolem theorem holds: if a set Γ of formulas of $\mathcal{L}2K$ has a faithful Henkin interpretation whose domain is infinite, then Γ has a faithful Henkin interpretation whose domain is countable (or the cardinality of K, whichever is larger). Every Henkin interpretation for $\mathcal{L}2K$ has an equivalent sub-interpretation whose domain is at most countable (or the cardinality of K, whichever is larger).

The upward Löwenheim-Skolem theorem also holds: if for each natural number n, a set Γ has a faithful Henkin interpretation whose domain has at least n members, then for each infinite cardinal κ, Γ has a faithful interpretation whose domain has at least κ-many members. The proofs of these theorems are straightforward adaptions of the usual constructions for first-order logic.[16]

As in the case of first-order logic, compactness is a corollary of completeness: let Γ be a set of formulas of $\mathcal{L}2K$. If every finite subset of Γ is satisfiable in a faithful Henkin interpretation, then Γ itself is satisfiable in a faithful Henkin interpretation. Recall that a set of sentences is categorical if all of its models are isomorphic to each other. Under Henkin semantics, we have that no theory with an infinite interpretation is categorical. Thus, second-order languages with Henkin or first-order semantics are not adequate to characterize infinite structures up to isomorphism.

7.4.2 Standard Semantics

Recall that standard semantics is equivalent to the restriction of Henkin semantics to full interpretations, structures in which the n-place predicate variables range over the collection of *all* sets of n-tuples of elements from the domain and the n-place functions range over the collection of all n-place functions on the domain. As noted, since full interpretations contain every relation and function, they certainly contain the functions and relations promised by the instances of the comprehension scheme and the axiom of choice (assuming separation and choice in the meta-theory). So full interpretations are faithful, and the deductive system D2 is sound for standard semantics.

Recall that a set of sentences is categorical just in case all of its models are isomorphic to each other. We noted above that with Henkin and first-order semantics, there are no categorical characterizations of any infinite structure. The crucial feature of standard semantics is the existence of categorical axiomatizations of the natural numbers, the real numbers, and a host of other mathematical structures. As we shall see, corollaries of these features include the *refutation* of compactness and the Löwenheim-Skolem theorems and, in light of Gödel's incompleteness theorem for arithmetic, the refutation of completeness.

The language of arithmetic has $A = \{0, s, +, \times\}$ among its non-logical terminology. The theory has first-order axioms stating that the successor function is

---

[16] See Shapiro (1991, pp. 89–95). As a historical note, the now-common Henkin proof of completeness was first discovered (and reported in Henkin (1950)) in the context of higher-order logic under (what is here called) Henkin semantics. The same proof was later adapted to provide a proof of completeness for first-order languages somewhat different from that given in Gödel (1930).

one-to-one, that zero is not the successor of anything, and the usual recursive definitions of addition and multiplication:

$$\forall x \forall y (sx = sy \to x = y) \land \forall x (sx \neq 0)$$
$$\forall x (x + 0 = x) \land \forall x \forall y (x + sy = s(x + y))$$
$$\forall x (x \times 0 = 0) \land \forall x \forall y (x \times sy = x \times y + x).$$

Then there is the *induction axiom*, a proper second-order statement:

$$\forall X [(X0 \land \forall x (Xx \to Xsx) \to \forall x Xx].$$

Let AR (for "arithmetic") be the conjunction of these axioms.

The intended model of AR is the interpretation $\mathbb{N}$ of $\mathcal{L}2A$ whose domain is the set of natural numbers and which assigns zero to 0, and assigns the successor function, the addition function, and the multiplication function to s, $+$, and $\times$, respectively. It is immediate that $\mathbb{N}$ satisfies AR. Moreover, any two interpretations of AR are isomorphic (see Shapiro (1991, pp. 82–83) or the original Dedekind (1888) for a proof). It follows that if M is any standard interpretation that makes AR true, then the domain of M is countably infinite. This entails that the upward Löwenheim-Skolem theorem fails for second-order logic with standard semantics.

It follows from the categoricity of second-order arithmetic that a sentence ϕ of $\mathcal{L}2A$ is true of the natural numbers (i.e., $\mathbb{N} \vDash \phi$) if and only if $AR \to \phi$ is a standard logical truth. That is, arithmetic truth is reducible to, or definable in terms of, standard second-order logical truth.

The proof of Gödel's incompleteness (Gödel (1931)) entails that the set of (first-order) truths of arithmetic is more complex than any set of theorems of a typical deductive system (see Boolos et al. (2002)). Second-order languages with standard semantics are thus inherently incomplete, in the sense that there can be no appropriate deductive system for it.

Compactness also fails. Let c be a constant symbol and consider the following set Γ of sentences:

$$\{AR, c \neq 0, c \neq s0, c \neq ss0, c \neq sss0, \dots \}.$$

Each finite subset of Γ is satisfiable in the natural numbers. But the entire set Γ is not satisfiable, since the denotation of c would have to be different from the denotations of 0, $s0$, etc. But, by the induction axiom and the categoricity result, the denotations of 0, $s0$, etc. exhaust the domain of each interpretation of AR.

This gives us a second refutation of completeness. Since the set Γ has no models at all, it would entail any sentence, say $0 = s0$. If there were a sound and complete deductive system for standard semantics, there would be a deduction of $0 = s0$ from members of Γ. But since deductions have to be finite, each deduction can have, as premises, only a finite number of members of Γ. So a finite subset of Γ would entail $0 = s0$. But, since each finite subset of Γ is satisfiable, it cannot entail this sentence.

The general notion of finitude cannot be captured in any language which satisfies the upward Löwenheim-Skolem theorem. If a theory in such a language has an interpretation of each finite cardinality, then it has an infinite interpretation. However, the notion of finitude can be expressed with a second-order language with no non-logical terminology (assuming standard semantics). The following purely logical sentence,

(FIN) $\forall f \neg (\forall x \forall y (fx = fy \rightarrow x = y) \wedge \exists x \forall y (fy \neq x))$,

asserts that there is no one-to-one function from the domain to a proper subset of the domain. So (FIN) is satisfied by an interpretation M if and only if the domain of M is finite.[17]

Finitude is one of a number of related notions that have adequate characterizations in second-order languages with standard semantics (usually involving no non-logical terminology) but cannot be characterized in any compact language, including second-order languages with Henkin or first-order semantics. Examples include countability, well-orderedness, well-foundedness, minimal closure, and the ancestral.[18] Any consistent attempt to formulate a characterization of any of these notions in a first-order or Henkin second-order theory will have unintended interpretations that miss the mark (see Shapiro (1991, Chapter 5, §5.1)).

All that remains is to refute the downward Löwenheim-Skolem theorem. In *real analysis*, the non-logical terminology includes $B = \{0, 1, +, \times, \leq\}$. The axioms are those of an ordered field, all of which are first-order,[19] plus a second-order statement of completeness, asserting that every non-empty, bounded set (or property) has a least upper bound:

$\forall X[(\exists y Xy \wedge \exists x \forall y(Xy \rightarrow y \leq x))$

$\rightarrow \exists x[\forall y(Xy \rightarrow y \leq x) \wedge \forall z(\forall y(Xy \rightarrow y \leq z) \rightarrow x \leq z)]].$

---

[17] Actually, (FIN) is satisfied by an interpretation M if and only if the domain of M is what is called "Dedekind-finite". The axiom of choice entails that Dedekind-finitude is equivalent to finitude.

[18] See Shapiro (1991) for definitions of these notions.

[19] The axioms for an ordered field are that addition and multiplication are associative and commutative, multiplication is distributive over addition, 0 is the additive identity, 1 is the multiplicative identity, every element has an additive inverse, every element but 0 has a multiplicative inverse, $\leq$ is a linear order, $0 \leq 1$, and the elements greater than or equal to 0 are closed under addition and multiplication.

Let AN (for "analysis") be the conjunction of the axioms of real analysis. The real number structure constitutes the intended interpretation, and AN is categorical (see Shapiro (1991, p. 84)). Since AN has an uncountable interpretation and no countable interpretations, the downward Löwenheim-Skolem theorem fails for second-order languages with standard semantics.

In first-order arithmetic, the (second-order) induction principle is replaced by a scheme. If ϕ is a formula in the language of first-order arithmetic, then

$$(\phi(0) \wedge \forall x(\phi(x) \rightarrow \phi(sx))) \rightarrow \forall x \phi(x),$$

is an axiom. The theory thus has infinitely many axioms.

Similarly, first-order real analysis is obtained by replacing the single completeness axiom with the completeness scheme,

$$(\exists y \phi(y) \wedge \exists x \forall y(\phi(y) \rightarrow y \leq x))$$
$$\rightarrow \exists x[\forall y(\phi(y) \rightarrow y \leq x) \wedge \forall z(\forall y(\phi(y) \rightarrow y \leq z) \rightarrow x \leq z)],$$

one instance for each formula ϕ of the language of real analysis that contains neither x nor z free.

The difference between, say, second-order real analysis and its first-order counterpart is that in the latter, one cannot directly state that every non-empty bounded set (or property) has a least upper bound. The closest one can come is a separate statement for each such set which is definable by a formula in the language of first-order analysis.

The same, or almost the same, goes for arithmetic and real analysis as formulated in a second-order language with Henkin semantics. To be sure, in those languages, the induction principle and the completeness principle are single sentences, with a second-order variable ranging over sets or properties. However, the only sets or properties that are guaranteed to exist in a given interpretation are the definable ones – and we only have those thanks to the explicit restriction to faithful interpretations, interpretations that satisfy each instance of the comprehension scheme. Without the restriction to faithful interpretations, we are not guaranteed the existence of any particular sets or properties. One who works in first-order arithmetic or analysis or one who invokes Henkin semantics on the respective second-order language (restricted to faithful interpretations) cannot apply the induction or completeness principle to a set or property until she shows that it is definable in the relevant language. The only difference between first-order arithmetic and second-order arithmetic with Henkin semantics is that a few more properties are definable in the second-order language than in the first-order language.

The first-order theory and the Henkin theory have interpretations which are not isomorphic to the real numbers. These are sometimes called *non-standard* interpretations. Indeed, the Löwenheim-Skolem theorems indicate that for every infinite cardinal κ, there are interpretations of first-order arithmetic and interpretations of first-order analysis whose domain has cardinality κ. The same goes for Henkin semantics. The study of non-standard interpretations has proven fruitful in illuminating the original informal theories.

Per Lindström (1969) showed that, in a sense, first-order logic is *characterized* by the meta-theoretic properties that distinguish it from second-order languages with standard semantics. Let $\mathcal{L}$ be any language/logic that is compact and has the property of the downward Löwenheim-Skolem theorem: if a theory is satisfiable, then it has an interpretation whose domain is at most countably infinite. Then $\mathcal{L}$ cannot make any distinction among interpretations that cannot be made with the corresponding first-order language (see Shapiro (1991, Chapter 6, §6.5)).

For better or worse, then, standard semantics is what makes second-order logic distinctive. The categoricity results and the concomitant failure of the limitative properties are the sources of both the expressive strength and the main philosophical and technical shortcoming of second-order logic.

Jon Barwise (1985, p. 5) once remarked:

> As logicians, we do our subject a disservice by convincing others that logic is first-order and then convincing them that almost none of the concepts of modern mathematics can really be captured in first-order logic.

And Hao Wang (1974, p. 154):

> When we are interested in set theory or classical analysis, the Löwenheim-Skolem theorem is usually taken as a sort of defect (often thought to be inevitable) of the first-order logic ... [W]hat is established [by Lindström's theorems] is not that first-order logic is the only possible logic but rather that it is the only possible logic when we in a sense deny reality to the concept of the uncountable.

The fact that second-order logic, with standard semantics, has rich, expressive resources invites the charge that second-order logic is just a branch of mathematics, and is not entitled to be called "logic" (see, for example, Quine (1986)). This is not the place to adjudicate this issue.

8 Intuitionism

Intuitionist logic rejects the law of excluded middle, that is, the law that says that $\phi \vee \neg\phi$ holds for any formula ϕ. Each instance of this sentence is a logical truth in all of the classical systems above. The rejection of excluded middle also requires eliminating some other classical laws of logic. In this section, we will explore some philosophical motivations for the theory, give a proof theory, and provide two options for a model theory for this logic, one of which is informal.

8.1 Philosophical background

8.1.1 Brouwer and Heyting on the Nature of Mathematics

L. E. J. Brouwer (1964b, p. 77) echoes the Kantian theme that a human being is not a passive observer of nature, but rather plays an active role in organizing experience:

> That man always and everywhere creates order in nature is due to the fact that he not only isolates the causal sequences of phenomena ... but also supplements them with phenomena caused by his own activity.

Mathematics concerns this active role. For Brouwer, the essence of mathematics is idealized mental *construction*. Consider, for example, the proposition that for every natural number n, there is a prime number $m > n$ such that $m < n! + 2$. For Brouwer, this proposition invokes a *procedure* that, given any natural number n, produces a prime number m that is greater than n but less than $n! + 2$. The proposition expresses the existence of such a procedure.

Brouwer's repudiation of some of the classical propositions and inferences flows from this constructive conception of mathematics. Consider, for example, the inference of double-negation elimination. Let P be a property of natural numbers and consider a proposition that there is a number n such that P holds of n; in symbols this is $\exists n Pn$. For an intuitionist, this proposition is established only when one shows how to construct a number n that has the property P. The negation of a proposition ϕ is established when one shows that the assumption of (the construction corresponding to) ϕ is contradictory. Thus, the double-negation $\neg\neg\exists n Pn$ is established when one shows that an assumption $\neg\exists n Pn$ is contradictory. Clearly, to derive a contradiction from the assumption that $\neg\exists n Pn$ is *not* to construct a number n such that Pn. Indeed, we can derive the contradiction and have no idea what such a number n might be. Thus, from Brouwer's perspective, double-negation elimination is invalid.[20]

---

[20] Consider the proposition that there are two irrational numbers a, b such that a^b is rational. Here is a non-constructive proof: let c be the square root of 2, which, of course, is irrational. If c^c is rational, then we are done: the square root of 2 is both of the indicated irrational numbers. If c^c is irrational, then $(c^c)^c$ is 2, and thus rational. This proof is not acceptable to an intuitionist, since it does not show how we can find the numbers a, b – it only shows that it is absurd that there are no such pairs. A constructive proof of this result is known.

On Brouwer's view, the practice of mathematics flows from mental introspection. A slogan of traditional idealism is "to exist is to be perceived." A corresponding slogan for intuitionism would be that in mathematics, "to exist is to be constructed." It follows from Brouwer's view that all mathematical truths are accessible to the mathematician, at least in principle:

> The ... point of view that there are no non-experienced truths ... has found acceptance with regard to mathematics much later than with regard to practical life and to science. Mathematics rigorously treated from this point of view, including deducing theorems exclusively by means of introspective construction, is called intuitionistic mathematics. (Brouwer (1964a, p. 90))

For Brouwer, every legitimate mathematical proposition directly invokes human mental abilities. Mathematical assertions are "realized, i.e. ... convey truths, if these truths have been experienced." As understood by an intuitionist, the principle of excluded middle amounts to a principle of omniscience: "Every assignment ... of a property to a mathematical entity can be judged, i.e., proved or reduced to absurdity." Brouwer's argument is that we are not omniscient and so we should not assume excluded middle. Heyting (1956) is largely responsible for taking Brouwer's mathematical ideas and turning them into a formalized system (perhaps against Brouwer's own wishes).

8.1.2 Dummett: Considerations on Language

Michael Dummett (1978b) provides a different motivation for the intuitionistic restrictions on logic. Unlike Brouwer, he focuses on linguistic matters. He explores the thesis that "classical mathematics employs forms of reasoning which are not valid on any legitimate way of construing mathematical statements ..." (p. 215). Dummett suggests that any consideration concerning which logic is correct must ultimately turn on questions of *meaning*. By its nature, language is a public medium, and as such, the meanings of the terms in a language are determined by how the terms are correctly used in discourse:

> The meaning of a mathematical statement determines and is exhaustively determined by its use. The meaning of such a statement cannot be, or cannot contain as an ingredient, anything which is not manifest in the use to be made of it, lying solely in the mind of the individual who apprehends that meaning... An individual cannot communicate what he cannot be observed to communicate: if an individual associated with a mathematical symbol or formula some mental content, where the association did not lie in the use he made of the symbol or formula, then he could not convey that content by means of the symbol or formula, for his audience would be unaware of the association and would have no means of becoming aware of it. (Dummett (1978b, pp. 216–217))

This view of language supports Dummett's *manifestation requirement*, a thesis that anyone who understands the meaning of an expression must be able to demonstrate that understanding through her behavior – through her use of the expression.

A typical semantics is *compositional* in the sense that the semantic content of a compound statement is a function of the semantic content of its parts. In the above model-theoretic semantics, for example, the truth (or satisfaction) conditions of a complex formula are defined in terms of the truth (or satisfaction) conditions of its subformulas. Dummett argues that this semantics runs afoul of the manifestation requirement. Consider, for example, an instance of excluded middle: $\phi \vee \neg \phi$. According to Dummett, one cannot understand the truth conditions for this in terms of the truth-conditions of its parts, since, according to the classical framework, one can know that the sentence is true without knowing which disjunct is true.

Dummett then argues that we can satisfy the manifestation requirement only if verifiability or assertability replaces truth (or satisfaction) as the main constituent of a compositional semantics. Presumably, language users can manifest their understanding of the conditions under which each sentence can be verified or asserted. In mathematics, verification is proof, since a mathematician can assert a given sentence only if she has proved it.

So instead of providing truth conditions of each formula, we supply *proof* conditions. As we shall see, the result is the repudiation of the validity of excluded middle and other inferences from classical logic.   •

8.1.3 Drawbacks

Much like the other alternatives we consider, intuitionism is not without its drawbacks. Most notably, many logicians are loath to reject excluded middle, which seems to be one of the more intuitive rules. Additionally, if one adopts intuitionistic logic to do mathematics, there are many classical theorems that cannot be proven.

8.2 Deduction

The formal language for (first-order) intuitionistic logic is the same as that of classical first-order logic. We turn to a deductive system D_I for intuitionistic logic. It is called *Heyting Predicate Calculus*. Recall that an *argument* is a non-empty collection of sentences in the formal language, one of which is designated to be the *conclusion*. We use "Γ," "Γ'," "Γ₁," etc, to range over sets of sentences, and we use "ϕ," "ψ," "θ," with or without subscripts, to range over single sentences of the language. We write $\Gamma \vdash_I \phi$ to indicate that ϕ is deducible from Γ in D_I. We write $\vdash_I \phi$ to indicate that ϕ can be deduced (in D_I) from the empty set of premises.

8.2.1 Heyting Predicate Calculus

All but one of the rules for our deductive system D for classical first-order logic carry over to D_I, and there is one new rule. As before, we define the deducibility relation by recursion, starting with a rule of assumptions:

- (As) If ϕ is a member of Γ, then $\Gamma \vdash_I \phi$.

There are two clauses for each connective and quantifier, indicating how to "introduce" and "eliminate" sentences in which each indicated symbol is the main connective. The glosses and motivations from the first half carry over.

- ($\wedge$I) If $\Gamma_1 \vdash_I \theta$ and $\Gamma_2 \vdash_I \psi$, then $\Gamma_1, \Gamma_2 \vdash_I (\theta \wedge \psi)$.
- ($\wedge$E) If $\Gamma \vdash_I (\theta \wedge \psi)$, then $\Gamma \vdash_I \theta$; and if $\Gamma \vdash_I (\theta \wedge \psi)$, then $\Gamma \vdash_I \psi$.
- ($\vee$I) If $\Gamma \vdash_I \theta$, then $\Gamma \vdash_I (\theta \vee \psi)$; if $\Gamma \vdash_I \psi$, then $\Gamma \vdash_I (\theta \vee \psi)$.
- ($\vee$E) If $\Gamma_1 \vdash_I (\theta \vee \psi), \Gamma_2, \theta \vdash_I \phi$ and $\Gamma_3, \psi \vdash_I \phi$, then $\Gamma_1, \Gamma_2, \Gamma_3 \vdash_I \phi$.
- ($\rightarrow$I) If $\Gamma, \theta \vdash_I \psi$, then $\Gamma \vdash_I (\theta \rightarrow \psi)$.
- ($\rightarrow$E) If $\Gamma_1 \vdash_I (\theta \rightarrow \psi)$ and $\Gamma_2 \vdash_I \theta$, then $\Gamma_1, \Gamma_2 \vdash_I \psi$.
- ($\neg$I) If $\Gamma_1, \theta \vdash_I \psi$ and $\Gamma_2, \theta \vdash_I \neg\psi$, then $\Gamma_1, \Gamma_2 \vdash_I \neg\theta$.

As with classical logic, by (As), we have that $\{A, \neg A\} \vdash_I A$ and $\{A, \neg A\} \vdash_I \neg A$. So by ($\neg$I) we have that $A \vdash_I \neg\neg A$. Recall that, in the classical case, we added a rule of "double-negation elimination" (DNE): if $\Gamma \vdash \neg\neg\theta$, then $\Gamma \vdash \theta$. This is the one rule from the classical deductive system D that does not carry over. Instead, we add an elimination rule for negation, like the one we introduced in Section 4, called *ex falso quodlibet* or, more colorfully, *explosion*:[21]

- ($\neg$E) If $\Gamma_1 \vdash_I \theta$ and $\Gamma_2 \vdash_I \neg\theta$, then for any sentence $\psi, \Gamma_1, \Gamma_2 \vdash_I \psi$.

Recall that each instance of this rule is derivable in the classical deductive system D, but that the derivation relies on double-negation elimination (DNE), which is not valid in D_I.

---

[21] In presentations of intuitionistic logic, it is customary to introduce a sentential constant $\perp$, for an absurd statement, and to define negation in terms of it: $\neg\phi$: $\phi \rightarrow \perp$. We would add an "elimination" rule for $\perp$: $\Gamma, \perp \vdash_I \psi$. It is straightforward to confirm that the above rule ($\neg$E) follows. Of course, the same move would work for classical logic. The next section concerns logical systems that demur from (EFQ).

The other clauses from the classical deductive system D carry over to D_I. Let θ be a formula, v a variable, and t a term. Then define $\theta(v|t)$ to be the result of substituting t for each free occurrence of v in θ.

- ($\forall$E) If $\Gamma \vdash_I \forall v\theta$, then $\Gamma \vdash_I \theta(v|t)$, for any closed term t.
- ($\forall$I) For any constant t, if $\Gamma \vdash_I \theta(v|t)$, then $\Gamma \vdash_I \forall v\theta$, provided that t does not occur in Γ or θ.
- ($\exists$I) For any closed term t, if $\Gamma \vdash_I \theta(v|t)$, then $\Gamma \vdash_I \exists v\theta$.
- ($\exists$E) For any constant t, if $\Gamma_1 \vdash_I \exists v\theta$ and $\Gamma_2, \theta(v|t) \vdash_I \phi$, then $\Gamma_1, \Gamma_2 \vdash_I \phi$, provided that t does not occur in ϕ, Γ_2 or θ.
- (=I) $\Gamma \vdash_I t = t$, where t is any closed term.
- (=E) For any closed terms t_1 and t_2, if $\Gamma_1 \vdash_I t_1 = t_2$ and $\Gamma_2 \vdash_I \theta$, then $\Gamma_1, \Gamma_2 \vdash_I \theta'$, where θ' is obtained from θ by replacing one or more occurrences of t_1 with t_2.

One final clause completes the description of the deductive system D_I:

- (*) That's all: $\Gamma \vdash_I \theta$ only if θ follows from members of Γ by the above rules.

8.2.2 Comparison with the Classical System D

It is immediate from the above that one can obtain the classical deductive system D from the intuitionistic one D_I by adding the rule of double-negation elimination (DNE): If $\Gamma \vdash \neg\neg\phi$ then $\Gamma \vdash \phi$. One gets the same result by adding any one of the following:

- The law of excluded middle (LEM): infer $(\phi \vee \neg\phi)$
  $\Gamma \vdash (\phi \vee \neg\phi)$.
- Classical *reductio*: if by assuming $\neg\phi$ one can derive a contradiction, then infer ϕ, discharging the assumption.
  If $\Gamma_1, \neg\phi \vdash \psi$ and $\Gamma_2, \neg\phi \vdash \neg\psi$, then $\Gamma_1, \Gamma_2 \vdash \phi$.
- Classical dilemma: if by assuming ϕ one can derive ψ, and if, by assuming $\neg\phi$, one can also derive ψ, then infer ψ, discharging both assumptions.
  If $\Gamma_1, \phi \vdash \psi$, and $\Gamma_2, \neg\phi \vdash \psi$, then $\Gamma_1, \Gamma_2 \vdash \psi$.

It is straightforward to show that any of these four items – (DNE), (LEM), classical *reductio* and classical dilemma – are equivalent to each other in D_I. First, one can derive any sentence in the form $\neg\neg(\phi \vee \neg\phi)$ in D_I. So an instance of (DNE) would yield (LEM).[22] Conversely, suppose we have (LEM). Take $\neg\neg\phi$ as an assumption. An instance of (LEM) is $(\phi \vee \neg\phi)$. We can derive ϕ by

---

[22] In effect, the derivation can be found in the first half, where we motivated (DNE) in the classical system.

(∨E), on the indicated instance of (LEM). The left disjunct is ϕ, and ϕ follows from the right disjunct via (EFQ).

If we had (LEM), then classical dilemma would follow, via a (∨E) on the relevant instance of (LEM). Conversely, if we had classical dilemma, then (LEM) would follow, since $(\phi \vee \neg\phi)$ follows from each of ϕ and $\neg\phi$, via (∨I).

Finally, suppose we had (DNE). If, by assuming $\neg\phi$, we can derive a contradiction, then we can infer $\neg\neg\phi$, by ($\neg$I). So we can infer ϕ by (DNE). So classical *reductio* holds. Conversely, suppose that classical *reductio* held. And assume $\neg\neg\phi$. If we further assume $\neg\phi$, we would have a contradiction. So ϕ holds, by classical dilemma, discharging the second assumption. Thus, we can infer ϕ from $\neg\neg\phi$. This is (DNE).

It is well known that in the classical deductive system D, the various connectives and quantifiers can be defined from each other. For example, one can derive $(\phi \rightarrow \psi)$ from $(\neg\phi \vee \psi)$ and vice versa; and one can derive $\forall x\phi$ from $\neg\exists x\neg\phi$ and vice versa. We could have just introduced, say, the connectives $\neg$ and $\wedge$, and the one quantifier $\forall$, and defined the others from those.

The various inter-definability derivations all fail in the intuitionist system D_I. For example, one can derive $(\phi \rightarrow \psi)$ from $(\neg\phi \vee \psi)$, but not vice versa; and one can derive $\neg\exists x\neg\phi$ from $\forall x\phi$, but not vice versa. So for intuitionistic logic, all of the connectives and quantifiers are necessary.

8.3 Informal Semantics: The Brouwer, Heyting, Kolmogorov (BHK) Interpretation

We now turn to giving two systems for the semantics of intuitionistic logic. We start with the more informal one.

As noted above, in ordinary semantics, one gives *truth conditions* for each sentence – the circumstances in which the sentence is true. This is manifest in the model-theoretic semantics for classical logic, where one gives *satisfaction* conditions for each formula, relative to an interpretation and an assignment to the variables. If the formula has no free variables, then we get truth conditions. We say what it is for a given sentence to be true in an interpretation.

The Brouwer, Heyting, Kolmogorov (BHK) interpretation replaces truth-conditions with *proof conditions*, or, more generally, verification conditions, in giving a recursive account of the semantics:

- Assume that we are told what counts as a proof of each atomic sentence. In elementary arithmetic, this would consist of a calculation.
- A proof of a sentence of the form $(\phi \wedge \psi)$ is a proof of ϕ and a proof of ψ.
- A proof of a sentence of the form $(\phi \vee \psi)$ is a proof of ϕ or a proof of ψ (and it is usually assumed that we know which).

- A proof of a sentence of the form $(\phi \rightarrow \psi)$ is a procedure that transforms any proof of ϕ into a proof of ψ.
- A proof of a sentence of the form $\neg\phi$ is a proof that there is no proof of ϕ.

The final clauses concern the quantifiers:

- A proof of a sentence of the form $\forall x \phi$ is a procedure that, given any n in the domain, produces a proof that ϕ holds of n.
- A proof of a sentence of the form $\exists x \phi$ is the construction of an object n and a proof that ϕ holds of n.

It is straightforward to verify, at least informally, that this semantics fits with the deductive system D_I in the following sense:

Theorem 8.1   *If* $\Gamma \vdash_I \phi$, *then there is a procedure that, given a proof of every member of* Γ, *produces a proof of* ϕ.

The proof goes by induction on the length of the D_I derivation.

Notice also that the rules and theorems of the classical system D that are not derivable in D_I do not seem to be sanctioned by the (BHK) semantics. Consider, for example, an instance of (LEM): $(\phi \vee \neg\phi)$. According to (BHK), a proof of this would be either a proof of ϕ, or a proof that there is no proof of ϕ. So, from the point of view of (BHK), the acceptance of every instance of (LEM) would amount to a statement that every sentence can either be proved or refuted. The (BHK) reading of (LEM) is that it is an unwarranted principle of omniscience.

Suppose that we had a proof of a sentence in the form $\neg\neg\exists x \phi$. According to the (BHK) reading, this is, in effect, a proof that there is no refutation of $\exists x \phi$. Prima facie, we can have that without thereby having a proof of $\exists x \phi$, for the latter requires the construction of an object n and a proof that ϕ holds of n. Consider, for example, the above classical proof that there are irrational numbers a, b such that a^b is rational (note 20 above). So double-negation elimination (DNE) does not seem to be sanctioned on the (BHK) semantics.

8.4 Kripke Frames

Finally, we consider a formal semantics. The reader should note that since the logic in the meta-theory in which the semantics is presented is classical, the results reported here would not be acceptable to an intuitionist. This semantics is a tool for a classical mathematician to study intuitionistic deduction.

A *frame* F is a triple $\langle W, a, \leq \rangle$ where W is a set of "worlds," $a \in W$, $\leq$ is a reflexive and transitive relation on W, and, for each $w \in W$, $a \leq w$. One might think of W as a set of possible states of information, and a as the actual state.

If $w \leq w'$, then w' is a possible continuation of w, or a possible future state of information of w.[23]

Let $F = \langle W, a, \leq \rangle$ be a frame. An *interpretation* on F assigns a classical interpretation to each world $w \in W$ – a domain of discourse and extensions for the non-logical terminology of the language, with the following provisos:

- If $w \leq w'$, then the domain at w is a subset of the domain at w'. In other words, as time moves on, new objects may be created, constructed, or discovered, but no object is ever destroyed. Once an object exists at a world, it continues to exist at all future worlds.
- Each constant denotes the same object in all worlds.
- If f is an n-place function letter, and $m_1, \ldots m_n$ are objects in the domain of a world w, then if $fm_1, \ldots m_n$ is p in w, then for all worlds w' such that $w \leq w'$, $fm_1, \ldots m_n$ is p in w'.
- If R is an n-place relation symbol, and if the sequence $m_1, \ldots m_n$ is in the extension of R in a world w, then for all worlds w' such that $w \leq w'$, $m_1, \ldots m_n$ is in the extension of R in w'.

These clauses entail that if an atomic sentence is true in a given state of information, it remains true in all future states.

Let $F = \langle W, a, \leq \rangle$ be a frame, and I an interpretation on F. Let $w \in W$ be a world in F, and let s be a variable assignment on w, a function from the variables to the objects in w.

We now say what it is for a formula ϕ to be *forced* in w by I under s:

- The clause for atomic sentences is the same as in classical model theory, but relativized to a world: $Rt_1 \ldots t_m$ is forced at w by I under s if and only if the sequence of objects denoted by $t_1 \ldots t_n$ is in the extension of R at w. And $u = v$ is forced at w by I under s if and only if the denotation of u and the denotation of v are the same.
- $(\phi \wedge \psi)$ is forced at w by I under s if and only if ϕ is forced at w by I under s and ψ is forced at w by I under s.
- $(\phi \vee \psi)$ is forced at w by I under s if and only if ϕ is forced at w by I under s or ψ is forced at w by I under s.

---

[23] Readers familiar with modal logic will recognize these as the frames for the modal logic S4 (see, for example, Hughes and Cresswell (1996)). This is consonant with the fact that sometimes S4 is thought to be the modal logic for knowability.

These two clauses are also the same as in the model theory of classical logic, but relativized to worlds. The next clauses make reference to other worlds in the frame.

- $(\phi \rightarrow \psi)$ is forced at w by I under s if and only if, for all worlds w' such that $w \leq w'$, if ϕ is forced at w' by I under s, then ψ is forced at w' by I under s. Less formally, this says that any future world that forces the antecedent also forces the consequent.
- $\neg\phi$ is forced at w by I under s if and only if, for all w' such that $w \leq w'$, it is not the case that ϕ is forced at w'. Less formally, this says that there is no future world in which ϕ is forced.
- $\forall x\phi$ is forced at w by I under s if and only if, for all worlds w' such that $w \leq w'$, ϕ is forced at w' by I under every assignment s' that agrees with s at every variable except possibly x.
- $\exists x\phi$ is forced at w by I under s if and only there is an assignment s' that agrees with s at every variable except possibly x such that ϕ is forced at w by I under s'.

The last clause is the same as in the model theory of classical logic, but relativized to worlds.

Note that the clauses for $\forall x\phi$ and $\exists x\phi$ are both strong. For the former to be forced, we must have that ϕ holds for all *present and future* objects. And for the latter, there must be an object that exists *now* (i.e., at w) such that ϕ holds of that object.

Notice that if the formula is a sentence, then the variable assignment plays no role. A sentence is forced in an interpretation under a variable assignment just in case it is forced in that interpretation under every variable assignment.

Theorem 8.2 (Monotonicity)   *If ϕ is forced at w by I under s and $w \leq w'$, then ϕ is forced at w' by I under s. In words, once a formula is forced, it stays forced in all future worlds.*

Theorem 8.3   *This semantics is sound and complete for intuitionistic logic. That is, if Γ is a set of sentences and ϕ is a sentence in the language, then $\Gamma \vdash_I \phi$ if and only if, for any interpretation I, any world w in I and any variable assignment (on the domain of w), if every member of Γ is forced at w by I under s, then ϕ is forced at w by I under s.*

See Kripke (1965) for proofs.

We close this section with a few examples of Kripke frames. Consider a frame with two worlds, a and w, with $a \leq w$, but not vice versa.

Philosophy and Logic

$$a \longrightarrow w$$

Figure 1: 2-world structure

The domain of both worlds is the singleton $\{0\}$. In the interpretation, 0 is not in the extension of a monadic predicate A at the base world a, but 0 is in the extension of A at w. Notice that $(A0 \vee \neg A0)$ is not forced at a (under any variable assignment). In particular, $A0$ is not forced at a, and neither is $\neg A0$, since $A0$ is forced at w. Also, $\neg\neg A0$ is forced at a, since $\neg A0$ is not forced at a and $\neg A0$ is not forced at w. But, again, $A0$ is not forced at a. So this interpretation undermines the inference of double-negation elimination (DNE).

Consider the following argument:

> If the Empire State Building falls, then somebody will be killed; therefore, there is someone who will be killed if the Empire State Building falls. Putting matters of tense aside, this can be symbolized: $(E \rightarrow \exists x K x)$, therefore $\exists x(E \rightarrow K x)$.

This argument is valid in classical logic. To establish it, first derive the instance of (LEM), $(E \vee \neg E)$, and then apply $\vee$E. However, the argument at least seems to be invalid. The premise is undoubtedly true. Yet, it does not seem that there is any particular person whose continued life depends on the Empire State Building not falling.

The argument is not valid in intuitionistic logic. Consider a frame with three worlds, a, w_1, w_2. We have $a \leq w_1$, but not vice versa, and $a \leq w_2$, but not vice versa.

Figure 2: 3-world structure

The domain of all three worlds is $\{c, d\}$, say, Carol and Dick. The sentence letter E is not true at a, but it is at w_1 and w_2. The extension of K is empty at a, it is the singleton $\{c\}$ in w_1 and it is the singleton $\{d\}$ in w_2. In words, the Empire State Building does not fall (yet) in the base world a, but it does in the other two worlds. In w_1, Carol is killed, and in w_2, Dick is killed. Notice that the premise $(E \rightarrow \exists x K x)$ is forced at the base world a: all of the worlds in the frame have it that if E, then somebody is killed. But the conclusion of the argument $\exists x(E \rightarrow K x)$ is not forced at the base world a. In particular, it is not forced at the base world that if the Empire State Building falls, then Carol will be killed (since Carol is not killed in w_2), nor is it forced at the base world that if the Empire State Building falls, then Dick will be killed (since Dick is not killed in w_1).

Consider the following frame: There are countably many worlds: $a, w_1, w_2, \ldots$ For each n, $a \le n$, but not vice versa, and if $n < m$, then $w_n \le w_m$, but not vice versa.

Figure 3: Countably-many-world structure

In the interpretation, the domain of the base world a is $\{0\}$, and the domain of w_n is the set of natural numbers less than or equal to n. There is just one monadic predicate letter A. The extension of A is empty at a, and the extension of A at w_n is the set of natural numbers less than n. The idea is that each world w_n has one new object, the number n, and that number goes into the extension of A at the next world w_{n+1}.

Notice that the sentence $\forall x(Ax \lor \neg Ax)$ is not forced at any world in this interpretation. For example, each world contains an object (0 at the base world a and n at w_n) that is not in the extension of A in that world, but is in the extension of A in the next world. So the following is forced at a:

$$\neg\forall x(Ax \lor \neg Ax).$$

This last is logically false in classical logic.

9 Paraconsistency: Demurring from *ex falso quodlibet*

The inference of *ex falso quodlibet* (EFQ) is that anything can be inferred from a contradiction: $\phi, \neg\phi \vDash \psi$. Although all of the logical systems presented in previous sections sanction (EFQ), many objections have been raised against it. In this section, we look at three types of logic that developed partly out of a desire to reject (EFQ).

Some reject (EFQ) on the ground that a conclusion of a valid argument must be *relevant* to its premises. Suppose, for example, that one starts with some premises Γ about human nature and facts about certain people, and then deduces both "Soy milk is really milk" and "Soy milk is not really milk." One can perhaps conclude that there is something wrong with the premises Γ, but should we be allowed to then deduce *anything at all* from Γ? Should we be allowed to conclude that "All cows are brown" and "The incompleteness theorem is incorrect"?[24]

---

[24] Advocates of classical (or intuitionistic) logic agree, of course, that drawing these inferences, in situations like this, would not be wise, but they insist that these are matters of pragmatic

Philosophical issues concerning the nature of logical consequence are involved. Roughly, since whether soy milk is milk has nothing to do with the status of the incompleteness theorems, some of those who hold that the premises and conclusion of a valid argument must have something to do with each other argue that we should not be able to move from "soy milk is milk" and "soy milk is not milk" to "the incompleteness theorem is incorrect." See Mares (2020) for a general overview of the motivations for relevance, or Dunn (2015), Mares (2004), or Tennant (2017), amongst others, for more detailed, specific, arguments.

Others object to (EFQ) on the ground that there are (or may be) some true contradictions, "paradoxical" statements that are both true and false (or true and not true). Consider, for example, Russell's paradox, which proved naive set theory to be inconsistent. Russell's paradox says that if we can make sets out of whatever we want, then we can form the set out of all of the sets which are not members of themselves. This set is such that if it is itself a member of itself, then it is not, and if it is not a member of itself, then it is! On most accounts, this type of contradiction causes a theory to "explode," essentially proving that everything is true. The proposal is to treat the existence of such a set as a "dialethia," a paradoxical sentence that is both true and not true. This allows one to preserve naive set theory, which allows us to make sets out of anything we would like. If there are such sentences, then (EFQ) is not truth-preserving – assuming, of course, that one does not also hold that every statement is both true and not true. For more developed arguments about dialethias, see Priest (1987), Priest et al. (2018) and Weber (2011), amongst others.

Logics that do not sanction the validity of (EFQ) are called *paraconsistent*. Lewis and Langford (1932) noted that in order to eliminate (EFQ), we also have to eliminate something else that is at least prima facie plausible. Consider the following derivation:[25]

    1. A
    2. $\neg A$
    3. $A \lor B$
    4. B

The first two lines are the premises of the argument. Line (3) follows from (1) by the rule of $\lor$-introduction ($\lor$I), and line (4) follows from (2) and (3) by disjunctive syllogism (DS).

---

advisability, not validity. Moreover, there might well be uses of (EFQ) when one is reasoning under assumptions.

[25] Martin (1986) shows that arguments like this were considered as early as the twelfth century. Note that this derivation of (EFQ) differs from the one given in the first half.

So, every paraconsistent logic must either reject (∨I), reject (DS), or reject the transitivity of deduction (i.e., the principle that it is acceptable to chain together valid arguments). The rejection of (∨I) is less common and is not considered here (but see Read (1988)). We consider three brands of paraconsistency: varieties of relevant logic, a dialetheic logic, and Neil Tennant's core logic. The first two reject (DS) and the third rejects the transitivity of deduction.[26] Each section gives details on motivations, a deductive system, and/or a model theory.

9.1 Relevance

9.1.1 Motivation

Anderson and Belnap (1975) argue that a given conclusion ϕ is a logical consequence of some premises Γ only if ϕ is *relevant* to Γ. Clearly, (EFQ) allows one to infer irrelevant conclusions. For example, from "it is raining" and "it is not raining" we can conclude "the moon is made of green cheese." So, according to Anderson and Belnap (1975), (EFQ) is not a valid inference form; it is a fallacy (see also Anderson et al. (1992), Read (1988), Mares (2020)).

The connective '→' of classical logic is sometimes called a "material conditional." Anderson and Belnap (1975, pp. 3–5) focus on so-called *paradoxes of material implication* as problematic features of classical logic. One such is $A \rightarrow (B \rightarrow A)$. Another is $A \rightarrow (B \rightarrow B)$. These are logically true in classical logic, but do not seem to match intuitions concerning conditional statements. These conditional tautologies seem to have less intuitive pull than other tautologies. For example, it seems distinctively odd to say that if it snows in Canada tomorrow, then if there is a rainbow in France, then there is a rainbow in France. At least part of this oddness (in addition to the general oddness of expressing a tautology) is that whether it snows in Canada tomorrow really has nothing to do with whether there is a rainbow in France. Other tautologies do not seem to have quite this feature (for example, it will either snow in Canada tomorrow or it will not snow in Canada tomorrow).

Examples like these highlight the fact that the material conditional does not accurately capture features of the conditionals of natural language. Anderson and Belnap wonder whether it should be called a conditional at all. They suggest that a conditional, properly so-called, should have something to do with *inference*.

---

[26] For other non-transitive logics, see Ripley (2015) and the work by the Buenos Aires logic group, including Barrio et al. (2021).

The paradoxes of material implication come in many shapes and sizes. A nice summary can be found in Kerr (2021, p. 4) (see also Priest (2001, section 7.5.3)). The following are among the list:

1. *Ex Contradictione Quodlibet*: $(\phi \wedge \neg\phi) \rightarrow \psi$.
2. *Ex Falso Quodlibet*: $\neg\phi \rightarrow (\phi \rightarrow \psi)$.
3. *Verum Ex Quodlibet*: $\phi \rightarrow (\psi \vee \neg\psi)$.
4. Positive Paradox: $\phi \rightarrow (\psi \rightarrow \phi)$.
5. Negative Paradox: $\neg\phi \rightarrow (\phi \rightarrow \psi)$.
6. Linear Order: $(\phi \rightarrow \psi) \vee (\psi \rightarrow \phi)$.
7. Unrelated Extremes: $(\phi \wedge \neg\phi) \rightarrow (\psi \vee \neg\psi)$.

We noted above that (EFQ) follows from the usual introduction rule for disjunction ($\vee$I), disjunctive syllogism (DS), and the transitivity of deduction, the thesis that deductions can be chained together at will. Anderson and Belnap, and their followers, demur from (DS), typically conceding the intuitive pull of this inference rule.[27]

Relevance logicians have advocated a wide variety of logical systems, and we make no attempt to survey them here. In this sub-section, we focus on deductive systems for the logics **E** and **R** of Anderson and Belnap and a sketch of a situation-semantics kind of model theory (as in Barwise and Perry (1983)).

Relevance logic is good at capturing whether a conclusion is appropriately related to its premises. It does have some drawbacks, though: we usually have to give up on some of the more intuitive rules of a system. For example, most relevant systems do not admit (DS). Anderson and Belnap even admit that this is a big sacrifice, but they maintain that since they can recapture it at the meta-level, it is not so bad (see footnote 27). Most relevance logics are in fact quite weak. For these reasons, amongst others, many classical logicians have opted to stick with their stronger logic.

9.1.2 Deduction

In previous sections, we presented natural deduction systems, invoking introduction and elimination rules for the connectives and quantifiers. Here we give Hilbert-style systems, consisting of axioms and very few rules of inference. We restrict attention to the sentential fragment of the logic.

The system **E** is supposed to be the logic of (relevant) entailment, and **R** is the logic of (relevant) implication. Both systems contain a relevant conditional,

---

[27] Anderson and Belnap note that there is a kind of meta-rule in line with (DS): if one can prove a sentence of the form $\phi \vee \psi$ and one can prove $\neg\phi$, then one can prove ψ. Anderson et al. (1992, pp. 498–502) note that this is a result of using classical logic in the meta-theory. The issues are complex and subtle.

but the conditional of **E** is meant to be strict (in the sense that it is only true if it is necessarily true). This makes **R** stronger than **E**. There are a whole series of relevance logics, each invoking different axioms (including some of those presented below). There is much debate about exactly which of these logics are correct, in some substantive sense. Some authors advocate for very weak logics (see, for example, Beall (2019), who holds **FDE** is correct, and Tedder (2021), who argues for **BB**). Others hold that logics even stronger than **R** are correct (see Avron (1990)). Because of this, there are whole families of relevance logics. For a detailed picture of them, and the relationships between them, see Øgaard (2016), who provides a map ordered by strength. The system **E** has the following rules and axioms (see Mares (2020)):

1. **Identity** $\vdash \phi \rightarrow \phi$
2. **EntT** $\vdash ((\phi \rightarrow \phi) \rightarrow \psi) \rightarrow \psi$
3. **Suffixing** $\vdash (\phi \rightarrow \psi) \rightarrow ((\psi \rightarrow \theta) \rightarrow (\phi \rightarrow \theta))$
4. **∧-elimination** $\vdash (\phi \wedge \psi) \rightarrow \phi, \vdash (\phi \wedge \psi) \rightarrow \psi$
5. **∨-introduction** $\vdash \phi \rightarrow (\phi \vee \psi), \vdash \psi \rightarrow (\phi \vee \psi)$
6. **∧-introduction** $\vdash ((\phi \rightarrow \psi) \wedge (\phi \rightarrow \theta)) \rightarrow (\phi \rightarrow (\psi \wedge \theta))$
7. **∨-elimination** $\vdash ((\phi \vee \psi) \rightarrow \theta) \leftrightarrow ((\phi \rightarrow \theta) \wedge (\psi \rightarrow \theta))$
8. **Contraction** $\vdash (\phi \rightarrow (\phi \rightarrow \psi)) \rightarrow (\phi \rightarrow \psi)$
9. **Distribution** $\vdash (\phi \rightarrow (\psi \rightarrow \theta)) \rightarrow ((\phi \rightarrow \psi) \rightarrow (\phi \rightarrow \theta))$
10. **Contraposition** $\vdash (\phi \rightarrow \neg\psi) \rightarrow (\psi \rightarrow \neg\phi)$
11. **Double-Negation** $\vdash \neg\neg\phi \rightarrow \phi$
12. **Modus Ponens** $\phi \rightarrow \psi, \phi \vdash \psi$
13. **Adjunction** $\phi, \psi \vdash \phi \wedge \psi$

The logic **R** is the same as **E**, with the following axiom replacing **EntT**:

Assertion $\vdash \phi \rightarrow ((\phi \rightarrow \psi) \rightarrow \psi)$.

It can be shown that the above paradoxes of material implication are not derivable in either of these systems.

9.1.3 A Sample Model Theory

We will give a kind of "situation semantics" here. There is considerable controversy over what, exactly, situations are. Sometimes a situation is thought of as a "part of a world" (Beall and Restall (2006, p. 49)), or as a "state of affairs" (Barwise and Perry (1983, p. 49)). They are also sometimes thought of as pieces of information (Urquhart (1972)). In any case, a situation is the sort of thing that makes sentences of a formal language true or false. For present purposes, it is crucial that, whatever they are, situations can be inconsistent.

Some technical features are invoked in the semantics:

1. There is a 3-place relationship on situations, R, roughly analogous to the usual two-place relation in the possible-worlds semantics for intuitionisic logic and modal logic. There is some controversy over how to interpret this relation (see Beall et al. (2012)). One thought is that $Rabc$ holds for situations, a, b, c, when the information of the situations a and b are contained in the situation c.
2. There is a "base" situation 0. Say that $a \leq b$ if $R0ab$.
3. There is a $*$-operator on situations, called the Routley star.[28] Again, there are a number of ways to interpret $*$; one such is that a^* is a maximal extension of a which is "compatible" with a.

Formally, this can be presented as follows (adapted from Anderson, Belnap, and Dunn (1992, §§48.3, 48.5)):

- A *frame* is a structure $(K, R, 0, *)$.
- K is a non-empty set – the collection of situations. We use $a, b, c, \ldots$ to range over elements of K.
- $0 \in K$.
- R is a three-place relation on K.
- $a^{**} = a$.
- If $Rabc$, then Rac^*b^*.

An *interpretation* on a frame is a relation $\models$ from K to the set of sentences of the language, with the following stipulations. Note that the clauses for conjunction and disjunction are very similar to those of classical logic and intuitionstic logic, but the clauses for negation and the conditional are quite different. This reflects the distinctive features of relevance logics:

- If ϕ is a sentence letter, then, if $a \models \phi$ and $a \leq b$, then $b \models \phi$.
- $s \models \phi \wedge \psi$ if and only if $s \models \phi$ and $s \models \psi$.
- $s \models \phi \vee \psi$ if and only if $s \models \phi$ or $s \models \psi$.
- $s \models \neg\phi$ if and only if $s^* \not\models \phi$.
- $s \models \phi \rightarrow \psi$ if and only if for every a, b, c, if $Rabc$, then either $b \not\models \phi$ or $c \models \psi$.

Different logics are obtained by placing restrictions on the accessibility relation R and the $*$-operation. The following frame conditions yield a sound and complete system for the logic **R** (Anderson et al. (1992, §§48.3, 48.5)):

1. $R0aa$.
2. If $Rabc$, then $Rbac$.

---

[28] See Routley and Routley (1972) and Routley and Meyer (1973).

3. A kind of associativity: if $\exists x(Rabx \wedge Rxcd)$ then $\exists x(Raxd \wedge Rbcx)$.
4. *Raaa*.
5. If *Rabc* and *R0aa'* then *Ra'bc*.

The conditions needed to get the logic **E** are significantly more complicated (see Anderson et al. (1992, §48.6)).

9.2 Dialetheism

Dialetheism is motivated by the idea that in order to resolve some paradoxes, we allow some sentences to be both true and false, or both true and not true. Consider, for example, the Liar (λ), a sentence which says of itself that it is not true:

λ: λ is not true.

Suppose we accept the usual, "naive" principle that a given sentence ϕ is true if and only if ϕ (with apologies for confounding use and mention). Then, using classical (or intuitionistic) logic, we are led to contradiction: we have λ if and only if $\neg\lambda$.

Within philosophy and logic, the most common reaction (by far) is to restrict the "naive" truth principle. Sometimes this is done in a way that does not even allow a Liar sentence to be formulated. Against this, the dialetheist proposes to accept the full truth-principle and to declare that the Liar, and other similar statements, are *dialetheias*: they are both true and not true. As noted above, this requires that disjunctive syllogism be rejected (unless the theorist somehow maintains that *every* sentence in the language is true (and false)): let A be both true and false, and B be just false (i.e., not also true). Then $A \vee B$ is true. And $\neg A$ is true. If (DS) were valid, then B would be true as well.

Admitting dialetheias has some further benefits: it allows us, for example, to pursue naive set theory (mentioned above). It also allows us to look at theories that are strong enough to be subject to Gödel's incompleteness theorems, but to still treat them as both complete and consistent (and, of course, as incomplete and/or inconsistent as well). However, as one might expect, many classical logicians have opted to stick with their original system because of the oddness of allowing sentences to be both true and not true.

We next provide the truth tables for the sentential fragment of Priest's "logic of paradox" (LP). Let us introduce a third truth-value I, in addition to truth (T) and falsehood (F). Here are the relevant truth-tables (see Priest (1979)):

∧	T	I	F		∨	T	I	F		¬	
T	T	I	F		T	T	T	T		T	F
I	I	I	F		I	T	I	I		I	I
F	F	F	F		F	T	I	F		F	T

The experienced reader will recognize these as the "strong Kleene" truth-tables, yielding the logic K3 (see, e.g., Gottwald (2020)). There, the truth-value I means something like "neither true nor false," and T is the only "designated" truth-value. Here, we think of I as "both true and false." So a sentence with value I is true (and also false). In LP, both T and I are "designated," they are both ways a given sentence can be true.

Validity, here and elsewhere, is the necessary preservation of truth. What is distinctive here is the dialetheic feature that I is a kind of truth. Let a *truth-value assignment* be a function from the sentence letters to the truth values $\{T, I, F\}$. For each truth-value assignment, the truth-tables generate a truth-value for every sentence of the language:

> $\Gamma \models \phi$ if and only if there is no truth-value assignment v such that $v(\phi) = F$ and for all $\psi \in \Gamma, v(\psi) \in \{I, T\}$.

We can recapitulate the above reasoning that neither (DS) nor (EFQ) is valid in LP in terms of the semantics. Consider a truth-value assignment in which A is I (both truth and false) and B is F (false only). Then $A \vee B$ is I, and so true, and $\neg A$ is I. But B fails to be true, so (DS) fails. Also $A \wedge \neg A$ is I, and so true, but B is F, so (EFQ) fails.

The language, so far, does not have a conditional. It is common to follow classical logic and define a "material conditional" as follows: $\phi \rightarrow \psi$ if and only if $\neg \phi \wedge \psi$. This results in the following truth-table:

→	T	I	F
T	T	I	F
I	T	I	I
F	T	T	T

On this picture, (→E), or modus ponens, is just an instance of (DS), and so is not valid. It must be admitted that this makes the logic rather hard to use, given how essential (→E) is. Priest (2006) develops an "intensional" conditional that does sanction (→E), as well as a contrapositive inference, but is still compatible with dialethism. We forego details.

9.3 Core Logic

Neil Tennant (1997) develops a *core logic* that is both paraconsistent, on general grounds of relevance, and intuitionistic (see also Tennant (2005)).[29] Tennant argues that this system better makes sense of mathematical reasoning. In mathematics, we rarely (for example) actually make use of (EFQ) to infer anything we want. Rather, when we find we have a contradiction, we go back and try to find where our premises went wrong. Core logic, argues Tennant, has an epistemic leg up on its peers: we either learn of a consequence that follows relevantly, or we learn that our original premises were inconsistent. In this way, Tennant claims that "our canon of deductive reasoning has been relevantized; but our powers of reasoning have been left intact" (Tennant (2005, p. 709)). Core logic is particularly good for automated deduction, as it accurately models actual computer processing.

Classical logicians typically reject core logic for one of two reasons. First, since it is non-transitive, its proofs can be very large, and in fact can be exponentially longer than their classical counterparts. Second, though Tennant does recover what is perhaps the intuition behind (EFQ), that something is wrong with the premises, he does not recover full, unrestricted, transitivity, and cannot make use of unrestricted Cut. Tennant does prove a meta-rule showing that core logic is transitive in certain instances, and these are the instances which Tennant holds are needed to recover all of mathematics.

The formal language of core logic is the same as that of classical logic as above, except that there is a primitive symbol $\perp$ for a contradiction. The introduction and elimination rules of core logic are similar to those of intuitionistic logic. We will note some of the differences here (but using the current framework for presenting inference rules). The rules for the quantifiers are the same as in classical and intuitionistic logic.

The rule for $\perp$ is:

- ($\perp$) $\Gamma, \phi, \neg\phi \vdash \perp$.

Recall the rule ($\vee$E) for both intuitionistic and classical logic:

- ($\vee$E) If $\Gamma_1 \vdash (\theta \vee \psi), \Gamma_2, \theta \vdash \phi$ and $\Gamma_3, \psi \vdash \phi$, then $\Gamma_1, \Gamma_2, \Gamma_3 \vdash \phi$.

In core logic (and classical core logic), this is bifurcated into cases:

- ($\vee$E)$_1$ If $\Gamma_1 \vdash (\theta \vee \psi), \Gamma_2, \theta \vdash \phi$ and $\Gamma_3, \psi \vdash \phi$, then $\Gamma_1, \Gamma_2, \Gamma_3 \vdash \phi$.
- ($\vee$E)$_2$ If $\Gamma_1 \vdash (\theta \vee \psi), \Gamma_2, \theta \vdash \phi$ and $\Gamma_3, \psi \vdash \perp$, then $\Gamma_1, \Gamma_2, \Gamma_3 \vdash \phi$.

---

[29] *Classical core logic* is obtained from core logic by adding the rule: if $\Gamma, \neg\phi \vdash \perp$, then $\Gamma \vdash \phi$.

- $(\vee E)_3$ If $\Gamma_1 \vdash (\theta \vee \psi), \Gamma_2, \theta \vdash \bot$ and $\Gamma_3, \psi \vdash \phi$, then $\Gamma_1, \Gamma_2, \Gamma_3 \vdash \phi$.
- $(\vee E)_4$ If $\Gamma_1 \vdash (\theta \vee \psi), \Gamma_2, \theta \vdash \bot$ and $\Gamma_3, \psi \vdash \bot$, then $\Gamma_1, \Gamma_2, \Gamma_3 \vdash \bot$.

Notice that disjunctive syllogism (DS) is acceptable: By the above rule ($\bot$), we have $\phi, \neg\phi \vdash \bot$. And, of course $\psi \vdash \psi$. So, by $(\vee E)_3$, $\phi \vee \psi, \neg\phi \vdash \psi$.

For some of the rules involving sub-derivations, one must actually use the assumption to be discharged. For example, in the above $(\vee E)$, one must use the assumptions ϕ and ψ in order to apply the rule. And, in each of the sub-derivations, the assumption cannot also be an undischarged assumption in the other sub-derivation.[30]

In core logic, all of the elimination rules require that the "major premise" (the sentence with the item to be "eliminated") must "stand proud," in the sense that it is a premise of the overall deduction, and not the conclusion of another rule. Another feature of the system is that some of the rules are presented in "parallelized" form. For example, $(\wedge E)$ is: if $\Gamma_1 \vdash \psi \wedge \psi$ and $\Gamma_2, \phi, \psi \vdash \chi$, then $\Gamma_1, \Gamma_2 \vdash \chi$. And at least one of the premises, ϕ, ψ must be actually used in the sub-derivation.

Recall from the first half that "Weakening" is the thesis that if $\Gamma_1 \vdash \phi$ and $\Gamma_1 \subseteq \Gamma_2$, then $\Gamma_2 \vdash \phi$. Theorem 4.2 shows that Weakening is a straightforward consequence of the way we present the rules for natural deduction, using "arbitrary" premise sets Γ. Weakening does not hold in core logic, since it allows irrelevancies to be introduced.[31]

Say that an argument $\langle \Gamma, P \rangle$ is *core valid* if either Γ just is $\{P\}$, or there is a derivation (in the foregoing presentation) of P from Γ in which every member of Γ is used. Of course, the core logician would just call this "valid."

All core derivations are in *normal form*, in the sense that there cannot be a deduction in which the conclusion of an introduction rule is the major premise for the elimination rule for the same connective.

As a result, the Cut rule is not valid in core logic:

$$\text{Cut } \frac{\Lambda, \phi \vdash \Theta \qquad \phi, \Theta \vdash \Gamma}{\Lambda, \Theta \vdash \Gamma}$$

Here, capital Greek letters are sets of sentences, and lowercase Greek letters are sentences. This implies that the universal transitivity of deduction (UTD) fails.

---

[30] Something similar holds for the rule of $(\rightarrow I)$: the consequent cannot be an undischarged assumption of the main derivation.

[31] Weakening also fails in relevance logics, but those are not presented via natural deduction. Tennant (1997) and (2005) use a style for presenting the deductive system that allows weakening to fail.

$$\text{(UTD)} \ \frac{\Lambda \vdash \Theta \qquad \Theta, \phi \vdash \Gamma}{\Lambda, \phi \vdash \Gamma}$$

This shows why the aforementioned derivation of (EFQ) from (DS) is blocked. In the application of (∨E), the major premise does not "stand proud," it is indeed the conclusion of the (∨I) rule.

The failure of (UTD) seems like a defect of the system. It precludes the common practice of using previously proved theorems and lemmas in proving new theorems. There is a danger that the resulting result cannot be normalized and thus be rendered as a core proof.

Tennant argues that there is a meta-theoretic result that attenuates this considerably. Suppose that some premises Γ entail a conclusion ϕ in intuitionistic logic (which, of course, is transitive). Then there is a set $\Gamma' \subseteq \Gamma$ such that either $\langle \Gamma', \phi \rangle$ or $\langle \Gamma', \bot \rangle$ is core valid.[32] Moreover, this result can itself be proven when the meta-logic is core logic, and so, in particular, it accords with intuitionism.

Tennant argues that this is a major *feature* of the system: "if the failure of unrestricted transitivity of deduction causes pain, it is fully assuaged by the resulting epistemic gain" (Tennant (1997, p. 344)). Tennant claims that one can improve many of the more usual derivations by showing that fewer premises are needed and/or that the premises are inconsistent.

Tennant (2015) provides a nice resolution of the Liar paradox, invoking core logic (or classical core logic). Suppose we add a truth predicate T to the language, with the naive rules:

$T\langle \phi \rangle \vdash \phi$
$\phi \vdash T\langle \phi \rangle,$

where $\langle \phi \rangle$ is a name of the sentence ϕ. Suppose also that there is a sentence λ that is equivalent to a statement of its untruth:

$\lambda \leftrightarrow \neg T\langle \lambda \rangle.$

One can derive a contradiction from these principles in intuitionisic (and thus classical) logic, in the familiar manner.

In core logic (and classical core logic), one can prove λ, i.e., $\neg T\langle \lambda \rangle$, from no other premises, and one can refute λ: $\neg T\langle \lambda \rangle \vdash \bot$. But these two derivations

---

[32] Also: suppose that some premises Γ entail a conclusion ϕ in classical logic. Then there is a set $\Gamma' \subseteq \Gamma$ such that either $\langle \Gamma', \phi \rangle$ or $\langle \Gamma', \bot \rangle$ in valid in classical core logic. In both cases, the result is a consequence of a more or less standard Cut-elimination procedure for (some) systems of natural deduction.

cannot be chained together to produce a derivation of ⊥. The result of this chain is not a normal proof, and the usual procedures to "normalize" intuitionistic (and classical) derivations do not terminate; they each result in an infinite loop.

9.4 Meta-theoretic Issues

As noted, the meta-theory for core logic is done in core logic. This is not the case for other paraconsistent frameworks, however. Typically, the meta-theory is classical. This leads to the strange result that (DS) and (EFQ) are both valid in the metalogic. Given that the logics in question are meant to be solving problems caused by (EFQ), it seems odd to have this problematic inference repeated "higher up."

Significant meta-theoretic results are few and far between. Though, as noted, there is a proof that the relevant logic **R** is sound and complete for the given semantics, most relevant logics do not fare so well. In fact, the semantics for relevant logic become increasingly complicated even for **E**, let alone the weaker logics. And Priest's LP does not have a decent proof-theory, so it is not even a candidate to be sound and complete, which means we do not have many meta-theoretic results to begin with. With LP, we have a good idea of what to make of truth, represented by the truth tables we gave, but not such a good idea of what to make of proof beyond that.

With the possible exception of core logic, the paraconsistent systems struggle to make sense of mathematical reasoning, though there is some work on capturing arithmetic in various relevance logics (see Logan and Leach-Krause (2021)). There is also some work on "inconsistent" mathematics (see Mortensen (2013)), but it does not mirror what we typically take to be mathematical practice.

10 Conclusion

We have provided the basics of classical first-order logic. This included developing the language, providing the syntax and model-theoretic semantics, and indicating some meta-theoretic results. We indicated that classical first-order logic has some significant drawbacks: it cannot characterize the natural numbers, or any other infinite structure, up to isomorphism, and it fails to capture some important and well-understood mathematical notions. To address this, and to help get a better understanding of the strengths and limitations of classical logic, we have considered classical, higher-order logic. When equipped with so-called standard semantics, this framework is very expressive, to the point that some argue that it is really mathematics, and not logic.

We also noted that some of the inferences of classical logic have been challenged, and we presented some rivals: intituionistic logic and some para-consistent logics. They also have drawbacks of their own, concerning the correctness of the disputed inferences. Of course, this is not the place to adjudicate the various disputes.

References

Anderson, A. R., and N. D. Belnap (1975). *Entailment: The Logic of Relevance and Necessity, Vol. I.* Princeton: Princeton University Press.

Anderson, A. R., N. D. Belnap, and M. Dunn (1992). *Entailment: The Logic of Relevance and Necessity, Vol. II.* Princeton: Princeton University Press.

Avron, A. (1990). Relevance and paraconsistency—a new approach. *Journal of Symbolic Logic 55*(2), 707–732.

Barrio, E. A., F. Pailos, and D. Szmuc (2021). Substructural logics, pluralism and collapse. *Synthese 198*, 4991–5007.

Barwise, J. (1985). Model-theoretic logics: Background and aims. In J. Barwise and S. Feferman (eds.), *Model-theoretic Logics*, pp. 3–23. New York: Springer-Verlag.

Barwise, J., and J. Perry (1983). *Situations and Attitudes.* Cambridge, Massachusetts, and London: MIT Press.

Beall, J. (2019). FDE as the One True Logic. In H. Omori and H. Wansing (eds.), *New Essays on Belnap-Dunn Logic.* Synthese Library (Studies in Epistemology, Logic, Methodology, and Philosophy of Science), vol 418, pp. 115–125. Cham: Springer.

Beall, J., R. Brady, J. M. Dunn, A. P. Hazen, E. Mares, R. K. Meyer, G. Priest, G. Restall, D. Ripley, J. Slaney, and R. Sylvan (2012). On the ternary relation and conditionality. *Journal of Philosophical Logic 41*(3), 595–612.

Beall, J., and G. Restall (2006). *Logical Pluralism.* Oxford: Clarendon Press.

Benacerraf, P., and H. Putnam (1983). *Philosophy of Mathematics.* Cambridge: Cambridge University Press.

Boolos, G. (1984). To be is to be a value of a variable (or to be some values of some variables). *Journal of Philosophy 81*(8), 430–449.

Boolos, G. (1985). Nominalist platonism. *Philosophical Review 94*, 327–344.

Boolos, G., J. Burgess, and R. Jeffrey (2002). *Computability and Logic*, 4th ed., Cambridge: Cambridge University Press.

Brouwer, L. E. J. (1964a). Consciousness, philosophy and mathematics. In P. Benacerraf and H. Putnam (eds.), *Philosophy of Mathematics: Selected Readings*, pp. 90–96. Englewood Cliffs, NJ: Cambridge University Press.

Brouwer, L. E. J. (1964b). Intuitionism and Formalism. In P. Benacerraf and H. Putnam (eds.), *Philosophy of Mathematics: Selected Readings*, pp. 77–89. Englewood Cliffs, NJ: Cambridge University Press.

Burgess, J. (1992). Proofs about proofs: A defense of classical logic. In M. Detlefsen (ed.), *Proof, Logic and Formalization*, pp. 8–23. London: Routledge.

Cocchiarella, N. (1988). Predication versus membership in the distinction between logic as language and logic as calculus. *Synthese 77*, 37–72.

Cook, R. T. (2002). Vagueness and mathematical precision. *Mind 111*(442), 225–247.

Corcoran, J. (1973). Gaps between logical theory and mathematical practice. In M. A. Bunge (ed.), *The Methodological Unity of Science*, pp. 23–50. Boston: Reidel.

Davidson, D. (1984). *Inquiries into Truth and Interpretation*. Oxford: Oxford University Press.

Davis, M. (1965). *The Undecidable*. Hewlett, New York: The Raven Press.

Dean, W. (forthcoming). *Skolem's Paradox and Non-absoluteness*. Cambridge: Cambridge University Press.

Dedekind, R. (1888). *Was Sind und Was Sollen die Zahlen?* F. Vieweg.

Dummett, M. (1978a). The Justification of Deduction. In *Truth and Other Enigmas*, pp. 290–318. Cambridge, MA: Harvard University Press.

Dummett, M. (1978b). The Philosophical Basis of Intuitionistic Logic. In *Truth and Other Enigmas*, pp. 215–247. Cambridge, MA: Harvard University Press.

Dummett, M. (2000). *Elements of Intuitionism*. Oxford: Clarendon Press.

Dunn, J. M. (2015). The relevance of relevance to relevance logic. In M. Banerjee and S. N. Krishna (eds.), *Logic and Its Applications*, pp. 11–29. Berlin Heidelberg: Springer.

Eklund, M. (1996). How logic became first-order. *Nordic Journal of Philosophical Logic 1*, 147–167.

Feferman, S. (2006). Predicativity. In S. Shapiro (ed.), *The Oxford Handbook of Philosophy of Mathematics and Logic*, pp. 590–624. Oxford: Oxford University Press.

Frege, G. (1879). *Begriffsschrift: Eine der Arithmetischen Nachgebildete Formelsprache des Reinen Denkens*. Halle a.d.S.: Louis Nebert.

Gilmore, P. (1957). The monadic theory of types in the lower-predicate calculus. In *Summaries of Talks Presented at the Summer Institute of Symbolic Logic at Cornell*, pp. 309–312. Princeton, NJ: Institute for Defense Analysis.

Gödel, K. (1930). Die vollständigkeit des axiome des logischen funktionenkalkuls. *Montatshefte für Mathematik und Physik 37*, 349–360. Translated as "The completeness of the axioms of the functional calculus of logic," in Van Heijenoort (1967), pp. 582–591.

Gödel, K. (1931). Über formal unentscheidbare Sätze der Principia Mathematica und verwandter systeme i. *Montatshefte für Mathematik und Physik 38*(1), 173–198. Translated as "On formally undecidable propositions of the Principia Mathematica," in Davis (1965), pp. 4–35, Van Heijenoort (1967), pp. 596–616, and Gödel (1986), 144–195.

Gödel, K. (1986). *Collected Works I*. Oxford: Oxford University Press.

Gottwald, S. (2020). Many-valued logic. In E. N. Zalta (ed.), *The Stanford Encyclopedia of Philosophy* (Summer 2020 ed.). <https://plato.stanford.edu/archives/sum2020/entries/logic-manyvalued/>.

Haack, S. (1978). *Philosophy of Logic*. Cambridge: Cambridge University Press.

Haack, S. (1996). *Deviant Logic, Fuzzy Logic: Beyond the Formalism*. Chicago: University of Chicago Press.

Henkin, L. (1950). Completeness in the theory of types. *The Journal of Symbolic Logic 15*(2), 81–91.

Heyting, A. (1956). *Intuitionism*. Amsterdam: North Holland.

Hughes, G. E., and M. Cresswell (1996). *A New Introduction to Modal Logic*. United Kingdom: Routledge.

Kerr, A. D. (2021). A plea for KR. *Synthese 198*, 3047–3071.

Kripke, S. (1965). Semantical analysis of intuitionistic logic I. In J. Crossley and M. Dummett (eds.), *Formal Systems and Recursive Functions*, pp. 92–130. Amsterdam: North Holland.

Lewis, C. I., and C. H. Langford (1932). *Symbolic Logic*. New York: Dover Publications.

Lindström, P. (1969). On extensions of elementary logic. *Theoria 35*(1), 1–11.

Link, G. (1998). *Algebraic Semantics in Language and Philosophy*. Stanford, CA: SCLI Publications.

Linnebo, O. (2017). Plural quantification. In Edward N. Zalta (ed.), *The Stanford Encyclopedia of Philosophy* (Summer 2017 Edition). https://plato.stanford.edu/archive/sum2017/entries/plural-quant.

Logan, Shay & Graham, Leach-Krouse (2021). On Not Saying What We Shouldn't Have to Say. _Australasian Journal of Logic_18 (5):524-568.

Löwenheim, L. (1915). Über möglichkeiten im relativkalkül. *Mathematische Annalen 76*, 447–470.

Marcus, R. (1995). *Modalities: Philosophical Essays*. New York: Oxford University Press.

Mares, E. (2004). *Relevant Logic: A Philosophical Interpretation*. Cambridge: Cambridge University Press.

Mares, E. (2020). Relevance logic. In E. N. Zalta (ed.), *The Stanford Encyclopedia of Philosophy* (Summer 2020 ed.). Stanford: Metaphysics Research Lab, Stanford University. https://plato.stanford.edu/entries/logic-relevance/

Martin, C. J. (1986). William's machine. *The Journal of Philosophy 83*(10), 564–572.

Montague, R. (1974). *Formal Philosophy: Selected Papers of Richard Montague*. New Haven: Yale University Press.

Moore, G. H. (1980). Beyond first-order logic, the historical interplay between logic and set theory. *History and Philosophy of Logic 1*, 95–137.

Moore, G. H. (1982). Zermelo's Axiom of Choice: Its Origins, Development, and influence. *Journal of Symbolic Logic* 49(2), 659–660. Springer-Verlag.

Moore, G. H. (1988). The emergence of first-order logic. In W. Aspray and P. Kitcher (eds.), *History and Philosophy of Modern Mathematics*, pp. 95–135. Minneapolis: University of Minnesota Press. Minnesota Studies in the Philosophy of Science Volume 11.

Mortensen, C. (2013). *Inconsistent Mathematics*. Mathematics and Its Applications. Netherlands: Springer.

Øgaard, T. F. (2016). Paths to triviality. *Journal of Philosophical Logic 45*(3), 237–276.

Peano, G. (1889). *Arithmetices principia: nova methodo exposita*. Bocca brothers.

Prawitz, D. (1974). On the idea of a general proof theory. *Synthese 27*(1), 63–77.

Prawitz, D. (2008). Meaning and proofs: On the conflict between classical and intuitionistic logic. *Theoria 43*(1), 2–40.

Priest, G. (1979). The logic of paradox. *Journal of Philosophical Logic 8*(1), 219–241.

Priest, G. (1987). *Doubt Truth to Be a Liar*. New York: Oxford University Press.

Priest, G. (2001). *An Introduction to Non-Classical Logic*. Cambridge: Cambridge University Press.

Priest, G. (2006). *In Contradiction: A Study of the Transconsistent*, 2nd ed., Oxford: Oxford University Press.

Priest, G., K. Tanaka, and Z. Weber (2018). Paraconsistent logic. In E. N. Zalta (ed.), *The Stanford Encyclopedia of Philosophy* (Summer 2018 ed.). Research Lab, Stanford University. https://plato.stanford.edu/entries/logic-paraconsistent/Metaphysics

Quine, W. V. O. (1986). *Philosophy of Logic*. Cambridge, MA: Harvard University Press.

Rayo, A., and S. Yablo (2001). Nominalism through de-nominalization. *Noûs 35*(1), 74–92.

Read, S. (1988). *Relevant Logic: A Philosophical Examination of Inference.* Oxford: Wiley-Blackwell.

Resnik, M. (1988). Second-order logic still wild. *Journal of Philosophy 85,* 75–87.

Resnik, M. (1996). Ought there to be but one logic? In B. J. Copeland (ed.), *Logic and Reality: Essays on the Legacy of Arthur Prior,* pp. 489–517. Oxford: Oxford University Press.

Restall, G. (2000). *An Introduction to Substructural Logic.* New York: Routledge.

Ripley, D. (2015). Naive set theory and nontransitive logic. *The Review of Symbolic Logic 8*(3), 553–571.

Routley, R., and R. K. Meyer (1973). The semantics of entailment. In H. Leblanc (ed.), *Truth, Syntax, and Modality: Proceedings of the Temple University Conference on Alternative Semantics,* pp. 199–243. North Holland.

Routley, R., and V. Routley (1972). The semantics of first degree entailment. *Noûs 6*(4), 335–359.

Rumfitt, I. (2015). *The Boundary Stones of Thought: An Essay in the Philosophy of Logic.* Oxford: Oxford University Press.

Russell, B. (1908). Mathematical logic as based on a theory of types. *American Journal of Mathematics 30,* 222–262.

Russell, B. (1973). *Essays in Analysis.* London: George Allen and Unwin Ltd.

Shapiro, S. (1991). *Foundations without Foundationalism.* Oxford: Clarendon Press.

Shapiro, S. (1993). Modality and ontology. *Mind 102,* 455–481.

Shapiro, S. (1996). (ed.) *The Limits of Logic: Higher-order Logic and the Löwenheim-Skolem Theorem.* United Kingdom: Routledge.

Shapiro, S. (1998). Logical consequence: Models and modality. In M. Schirn (ed.), *The Philosophy of Mathematics Today,* pp. 131–156. Oxford: Clarendon Press.

Shapiro, S., and T. Kouri Kissel (2020). Classical logic. In E. N. Zalta (ed.), *The Stanford Encyclopedia of Philosophy* (Winter 2020 ed.). Metaphysics Research Lab, Stanford University. https://plato.stanford.edu/entries/logic-classical/

Stebbing, L. S. (1939). *Thinking to Some Purpose.* London: Penguin Books.

Tarski, A. (2002). On the concept of following logically. *History and Philosophy of Logic 23,* 155–196.

Tedder, A. (2021). Information flow in logics in the vicinity of BB. *The Australasian Journal of Logic 18,* 1–24.

Tennant, N. (1997). *The Taming of the True*. New York: Oxford University Press.

Tennant, N. (2005). Relevance in reasoning. In S. Shapiro (ed.), *The Oxford Handbook of Philosophy of Mathematics and Logic*, pp. 696–726. Oxford: Oxford University Press.

Tennant, N. (2015). A new unified account of truth and paradox. *Synthese 124*, 571–605.

Tennant, N. (2017). *Core Logic*. Oxford: Oxford University Press.

Urquhart, A. (1972). Semantics for relevant logics. *The Journal of Symbolic Logic 37*(1), 159–169.

Van Heijenoort, J. (1967). *From Frege to Gödel*. Cambridge, MA: Harvard University Press.

Wang, H. (1974). *From Mathematics to Philosophy*. London: Routledge and Kegan Paul.

Weber, Z. (2011). A paraconsistent model of vagueness. *Mind 119*(476), 1025–1045.

Whitehead, A. N., and B. Russell (1910). *Principia Mathematica*. Cambridge: Cambridge University Press.

Woods, C. (2021). An introduction to reasoning. https://sites.google.com/site/anintroductiontoreasoning/ Accessed: March 2nd 2021.

Cambridge Elements ≡

Philosophy and Logic

Bradley Armour-Garb

SUNY Albany

Brad Armour-Garb is chair and Professor of Philosophy at SUNY Albany. His books include *The Law of Non-Contradiction* (co-edited with Graham Priest and J. C. Beall, 2004), *Deflationary Truth and Deflationism and Paradox* (both co-edited with J. C. Beall, 2005), *Pretense and Pathology* (with James Woodbridge, Cambridge University Press, 2015), *Reflections on the Liar* (2017), and *Fictionalism in Philosophy* (co-edited with Fred Kroon, 2020).

Frederick Kroon

The University of Auckland

Frederick Kroon is Emeritus Professor of Philosophy at the University of Auckland. He has authored numerous papers in formal and philosophical logic, ethics, philosophy of language, and metaphysics, and is the author of *A Critical Introduction to Fictionalism* (with Stuart Brock and Jonathan McKeown-Green, 2018).

About the Series

This Cambridge Elements series provides an extensive overview of the many and varied connections between philosophy and logic. Distinguished authors provide an up-to-date summary of the results of current research in their fields and give their own take on what they believe are the most significant debates influencing research, drawing original conclusions.

Printed in the United States
by Baker & Taylor Publisher Services